THE ESSENTIAL

Alberta Driver's Licence Handbook

ELS SERIES

KNOWLEDGE, IN EVERY LANE

ElS series identifies as an independent third-party seller that aims to help test takers achieve their goals by providing **valuable lessons** that take inspiration from **The Alberta Vehicle Code**, **Various official sources** and our **expertise.** Also, via **200 questions and answers** that are the most closest to the real exam questions.

We are by no means an **official source**, a **copy** or **our own version** of the **Official Alberta Driver's Handbook** nor **designed to replace it** in any shape or form.

ISBN: 9798788573731

CBMA09012201

THE ESSENTIAL ALBERTA DRIVER'S LICENSE HANDBOOK

Foreword

The journey to becoming a licensed driver can be both exciting and nerve-wracking. What's more, the importance of being a licensed driver is immense.

For this reason, we've created the Essential a Province-specific collection of handbooks designed to help you confidently pass your driver's license knowledge test and embark on a lifetime of safe and responsible driving.

Our main objective is to prepare you thoroughly for the exam so that you don't face any difficulties during the test by making your preparation accurate and a fun experience.

QUESTIONS AS SEEN ON THE TEST:

Our dedicated team of experts has carefully curated a collection of practice questions that closely resemble those you'll encounter on test day.

Drawing on the structure of past questions, we've designed our questions to reflect real-world scenarios, helping you build the confidence and knowledge needed to tackle any challenge the test may throw your way.

CONCISE LESSONS:

This book offers concise, high-quality lessons on traffic laws, road signs, and safe driving practices.

Our engaging storytelling approach makes complex road rules and signals easy to understand, allowing you to quickly grasp the essential information you need to pass your knowledge test and become a skilled and responsible driver.

EXPLAINED ANSWERS:

To help you build a solid foundation of driving knowledge, each practice question in our material explains the correct answer.

fully grasping the reasoning behind each answer will help you better comprehend the subject at hand—improving your ability to tackle more complex topics in the future.

YOUR PROVINCE, YOUR RULES:

Each book in the Essential is written to cater to each Province's unique rules and regulations.

Moreover, learning should be relevant and engaging, which is why our handbooks focus on the information that matters most to you.

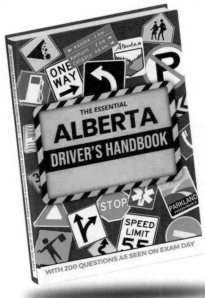

THANK YOU FOR TRUSTING ELS SERIES

Dear Future Drivers, thank you for choosing ELS SERIES.

We are truly grateful that you've chosen The Essential as your trusted guide to becoming a skilled driver. In a world filled with countless options, we're honoured that you've trusted our study aid book to support your quest to become a licensed driver. Your determination to become an exceptional driver is inspiring, and we're thrilled to be a part of it.

The Essential team has dedicated their hearts, expertise, and passion to crafting this book series with one goal and one goal only: helping you get your driver's license in the best (and easiest!) way possible. We understand the learning challenges you're facing and are committed to serving as steadfast companions you can lean on every step of the way.

Your trust in us means the world, and we truly value you as our customer. Thank you for choosing Us, and here's to a bright future on the open road!

Warmly,

THE ELS SERIES TEAM

SCAN ME

FOR MORE AMAZING PRODUCTS, VISIT OUR AMAZON AUTHOR PAGE BY SCANNING THIS QR CODE

ELS SERIES

THE ESSENTIAL ALBERTA DRIVER'S HANDBOOK

Contents   Page

THE ESSENTIAL ALBERTA DRIVER'S HANDBOOK

Content	Page

The Province of Alberta acknowledges that the freedom and mobility given by a driver's license is a vital aspect of most Albertans' quality of life. Along with this obligation, the province of Alberta wishes to maintain all driver's licenses valid for as long as it is safe for them to do so. This is why an adequate testing system takes place to determine whether or not a person is capable of driving a specific type of vehicle.

In Alberta, it takes candidates at least 3 years to get a **full, non-GDL Class 5** Licence. A process that consists of 3 stages, the Class 7 Licence or the learner licence. The Class 5-GDL Licence is also known as the probationary licence and finally, the Class 5 Licence is commonly referred to as the Full, non-GDL driver's licence.

This multi-stage driver licensing process is known as the **Learner or Graduated Driver License GDL Program**. Giving the motorists a chance to gradually improve their driving skills and extend their practice driving time. Participation in the GDL program **is mandatory for all new drivers, regardless of their age.**

The services of driver's licenses are offered through the Alberta registry agent network and **Only individuals who are residents of Alberta** are eligible to obtain a driver's license.

If the applicant is not from Canada or the United States, they must provide valid immigration papers to be regarded as residents.

The Alberta driver's licence

You need to realize that driver's licenses are tailored to the class/type of vehicle a person intends to operate; in most cases, applicants are individuals who want to drive standard passenger vehicles, pickup trucks, or vans. Hence, the Class 5 driver's licence is in the province of Alberta.

The Alberta driver's licence is issued in accordance with the Traffic Safety Act. It is mandatory for individuals to possess their driver's license while driving a motor vehicle.

Upon the request of a police officer, individuals operating a motor vehicle must present **their valid driver's license, along with insurance and registration documents.**

New Alberta residents are permitted to utilize their valid driver's license from another jurisdiction for the **initial 90 days of residency.** Within this period, individuals are required to apply for an Alberta driver's license and surrender their previous license to an Alberta registry agent office. **To qualify as a resident,** a person must have the legal right to stay in Canada, reside in Alberta, and typically be physically present in Alberta.

You are required to renew your driver's license by the expiration date. In case you lose your driver's license, or if it gets destroyed, stolen, or unreadable, you need to apply for the replacement on an immediate basis at the registry agent's office.

If you possess a valid driver's license from one of the countries listed below, you can obtain your Alberta license **without undergoing a knowledge or road test:** Australia, Austria, Belgium, France, Germany, Japan, Republic of Korea, Switzerland, Taiwan, United Kingdom, and the United States. Nevertheless, To exchange a license from a country that doesn't have an agreement, you'll need to pass these tests in Alberta.

THE TESTING PROCESS

If you wish to get your driver's license in the province of Alberta, you must follow this testing process :

1. **Meeting the vision requirements**

2. **Passing the Knowledge test**

3. **Passing the Behind the wheel test**

VISION REQUIREMENTS

Before you can receive an Alberta Driver's Licence, you must undergo a vision assessment. If your vision does not meet the required standards, you will be directed to an optometrist or ophthalmologist to fill out a Vision Referral form. Remember to bring your corrective glasses or contact lenses with you for the assessment.

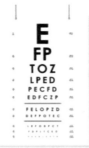

The optometrist will ask you to read lines of letters with both eyes open at first, then with each eye separately. Each phase of the exam will be guided by the employee.

If a driver wears glasses or contact lenses, their license will have a restriction requiring them to wear them while operating a vehicle.

THE KNOWLEDGE TEST

In order to drive legally in the province of Alberta you need to successfully pass a knowledge test that assesses your understanding of traffic control signs and signals as well as the rules of the road and your ability to comprehend and show responsible behaviour as a legal driver.

Passing the knowledge test is an important step in acquiring your driver's licence. This is a written examination that assesses your understanding of **Road signs** and **traffic laws and regulations** in your state or province.

The Alberta provincial knowledge test consists of :

- **30 multiple-choice** questions

- you must properly answer at least **25 of them** to pass.

- all knowledge tests are **now computer-based** rather than paper-based.

Note that the permit you receive as you pass isn't an actual driver's licence

The questions on your knowledge exam will cover: Seat Belt Laws, Traffic Control, Vehicle Control, Lane Control, Speed Limits, Turns, Yielding the Right-of-way, Restrictions, Parking, Maintaining Attention, Headlight Use, Signaling, Licensing & Insurance

THE ROAD TEST

To demonstrate that you can safely operate a motor vehicle by adhering to the rules of the road, you will be evaluated on your driving skills in a basic road test. The successful completion of the basic road test enables GDL drivers to upgrade their licenses from class 7 (Learner) to class 5-GDL.

During the probationary period that follows, you will have a minimum of two years to continue enhancing your driving skills in preparation for the advanced road test, which is required to exit the GDL program.

This basic road test lasts around 30 minutes and includes pre-test instructions from the examiner, as well as a review of your test results.

What's after passing this basic test? **The advanced road test,** it evaluates whether a probationary driver has acquired the essential advanced driving skills and experience in demanding conditions to qualify for full licensure.

Successfully passing this test is a prerequisite for transitioning out of the Graduated Licensing Program and attaining the status of a full class 5 (non-GDL) driver. The duration of this road test **is approximately 60 minutes**.

On the driving test, you will do the following maneuvers:

Right-of-Way: Allow pedestrians to cross the street, pull over and stop for emergency vehicles, and avoid entering intersections where you will obstruct other traffic.

Straight-In Parking: When parked properly, the car should be centered within the area, with no part of the vehicle projecting into the traffic lane.

Approach of an intersection: Get into the correct lane and look in all directions.

Parking on a Grade: Uphill and downhill parking, with and without a curb.

Backing : Back for a distance of 50 feet at a slow pace while looking back. Use neither the rear-view mirror nor the rear-view camera monitor.

Three-Point Turn: Turn the vehicle around in a 20-40 foot space.

Traffic Signals: Get into the proper lane and approach the light at a slow enough pace to allow you to stop if the light changes. When the signal turns green, wait until all other traffic has cleared the junction before proceeding.

Stop signs: Approach in the proper lane, come to a complete stop before the stop line or crossing and remain halted until you may safely advance.

Using signals while turning: Enter the proper lane and indicate your turn for the final 100 feet. Hand signals and mechanical signals are both acceptable.

Passing: Always keep an eye ahead and behind you to ensure a safe passage.

Following safely: Avoid driving too closely behind other vehicles. minimize the following.

Staying on the proper lane: With the exception of one-way streets, stay in the right lane.

The proper driving posture: Don't rest your elbow in the window and keep both hands on the wheel.

LEARNER'S LICENCE RESTRICTIONS

Parental consent requirement:

If you are less than 18 years of age and are applying for the driving licence, your legal guardian or parent, who must provide the proof of guardianship, should go along with you to the registry office in order to sign the consent on the application of your licence. Your guardians or parents have the right to withdraw their consent in writing any time they want until you are 18 years old.

Restrictions placed on your licence:
You are not allowed to drive between the period **of 12:00 am, and 5:00 am,** When driving, you need to **have 0% alcohol levels(Zero Tolerance)**, The number of people in your vehicle must be equal to or less than the number of seat belts in your vehicle.

If you don't obey these restrictions as a GDL driver, **2 demerit points** will be added to your driving record.

Before getting a suspension of your license, you will be allowed 8 demerit points.

TRAFFIC SIGNAL RULES

Traffic at intersections may be controlled by utilizing **traffic signals** that employ green, yellow, and red lights. Whichever lane of traffic has **the right-of-way** is determined by the colour of the light. A horizontal or vertical traffic signal may be used.

 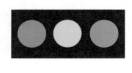

RED LIGHT

In the event of a **solid red light,** drivers are required to come to a **full stop** (before the stop line or crosswalk). This rule applies at any intersection even where there is no crosswalk or stop line. To avoid accidents, drivers must wait for the green light before proceeding through the intersection.

PROCEEDING AT A RED LIGHT

 The first thing you need to know is if **turning right at a red light** is allowed in the location where you drive.

In the Province of Alberta, right turns on red **are allowed** if they can be accomplished safely unless a **road sign** indicates otherwise.

After a full stop, yield to other traffic and pedestrians on both your lane and the right lane crosswalk.

The only left turn authorized at a **red light** is into a **one-way street from a one-way street** unless a sign prohibits the turn. To make this turn, drivers must bring their vehicles to a full stop, and only then may they proceed.

FLASHING RED LIGHT

When facing a **flashing red light** put your vehicle to a complete stop, look for traffic from all sides of the intersection ahead, and if clear you can then proceed.

The easiest way to deal with flashing red lights is **to treat them as stop signs,** Always come to a full stop, check the intersection and yield the right of way to others who got to the intersection before you, and then proceed when the way is clear.

GREEN ARROW WITH RED LIGHT

When confronted with a traffic signal that has both a green arrow and a red control light, drivers may pass through the intersection **only in the direction indicated by the arrow** without stopping.

YELLOW LIGHT

Yellow lights mean that you need to come to a full stop. Unless you are closer than one vehicle length to the intersection, then you are going to proceed through. do it defensively by covering the brakes, making sure you are scanning the intersection and that there aren't any road users. If you are farther back from the intersection than one vehicle length you need to come to a full stop.

FLASHING YELLOW LIGHT

flashing yellow light needs to be treated similarly **to a yield sign.** Continue cautiously after allowing pedestrians to cross and other vehicles to pass. You should slow down but not stop if there is no traffic on your way.

GREEN LIGHT

If the traffic control light is solid green, drivers may go through the intersection without stopping or slowing down if they drive within the speed limit, unless they must yield to **oncoming vehicles** when **turning left** or to **pedestrians in the crosswalk** when turning right or left.

When turning left, start by getting into the leftmost of the lane to get ready to take the left-hand turn,

as you get closer to the intersection check that there is no oncoming traffic that you may obstruct and then also make sure that no pedestrians are crossing or about to cross. While arriving at the intersection, check your rear-view mirror as well as your left-side mirror and blind spots. You can then proceed to make the left turn accurately.

FLASHING GREEN LIGHT

A flashing green light is **rarely used** and can mean two things, either you can move forward freely as traffic at the intersection will be free because **all directions are stopped by a red light,** and therefore, there is less risk for obstruction. Or it can mean that the signal can be **pedestrian-activated**, thus use extra caution.

GREEN ARROW WITH GREEN LIGHT

Drivers are not obliged to yield to the arrow's direction when encountering a traffic light displaying both a green arrow and a solid green traffic control light. In instances where it is safe and legal, drivers facing the green light are also permitted to travel in the opposite direction.

Remember: If you are approaching an intersection and the traffic lights are **not working**, you should treat it as **a 4-way stop sign** intersection and apply the suitable right-of-way rules *(See Page 36)*.

There are some different types of yield signs that you may observe as per your Province rules, some would even ask you to **yield on solid green or yellow lights**. Be cautious when you encounter these signs on the road.

PEDESTRIAN SIGNALS AND SIGNS

Pedestrian safety is a priority for the Province of Alberta. In order to anticipate the activities of others with whom you share the road, drivers must be familiar with pedestrian control signals. When it is safe to do so, pedestrians facing a traffic light with the word **"WALK"** or a similar symbol may cross the road. As long as the word or symbol appears, pedestrians may continue to cross and clear the intersection. **Countdown timers** may be seen on certain pedestrian signals to let pedestrians know how much time is left before the light changes.

If the text or symbol **"DON'T WALK"** appears on a traffic light, then a pedestrian must not cross the intersection.

 "WALK" is signalled by this pedestrian signal.

 "DON'T WALK" or "WAIT" signs for pedestrians

 When the flashing **"DON'T WALK"** or the flashing upraised hand begins:

A. If you are already in the street, proceed to finish crossing.
B. If you have not yet left the curb, refrain from starting to cross.

School zones or areas, playground zones or areas, school crossings, and pedestrian crossings all have yellow lights on a sign with a symbol to convey caution. Drivers must slow down to a maximum of 30 km/h while the yellow lights are flashing and yield or stop for pedestrians.

Pedestrian crossing signs with **yellow lights.**

Pedestrians must follow the regulations for the colour of light they are facing at intersections with traffic control signals that lack pedestrian **WALK** and **DON'T WALK** signals.

• *Red light*; Do not cross the street at this time.

• *Yellow light*; Avoid entering the junction if you're already there.

• *Green light*; Proceed, Any designated or unmarked crosswalks may be used to cross the street.

Pedestrians should always look both ways before crossing the street.

IMPORTANT: The common signs that a pedestrian crossing the road is blind include carrying a **white cane** and being accompanied by a **guide dog**

Lane reversals are employed to manage traffic flow in specific lanes, with reversible lanes being a common application. Reversible lanes, which adjust traffic direction based on the time of day, often utilize this control. The signal(s) in one or more lanes transition from a red X to a green or yellow arrow.

SOLID RED X:

 Drivers must not enter or stay in a driving lane marked with a **solid red X.** An impending traffic signal is shown by this light. The green arrow indicates that the lane is safe to enter.

DOWNWARD POINTING GREEN ARROW

 Driving in the lane with the **downward-pointing green arrow** is authorized for drivers facing the arrow's.

YELLOW ARROW DOWN TO THE LEFT OR RIGHT

 This traffic signal simply means that this lane is **about to be closed**, therefore safely merge into the direction of the arrow and give the way to vehicles already present.

ROAD SIGNS

Road signs come in various shapes and colours, and memorizing the significance of each traffic sign can be challenging for some road users.

Nevertheless, studying them and understanding what each category is supposed to mean based on colours and shapes is a key point toward a quicker understanding of what you are being demanded to do for optimal safety.

Traffic signs convey information to road users via 3 variables

A. The colour of the sign
B. The shape of the sign
C. The symbols and/or writing on the sign

COLOUR CODING

 RED :
A Prohibition or a stop sign
The adoption of the red colour on traffic signs is defined as a stop, a yield, or a prohibition.

 YELLOW :
Warning of a danger or a caution
Some signs are coloured yellow, those should be perceived as a warning.

 GREEN :
Announce traffic movement and directional instructions

The green signs are most recurrently presented on highways and freeways and they mainly show travelers the directions, the exits, or the attractions.

ORANGE :

Temporary signs often alert travellers about construction and maintenance

The orange road signs refer to temporary conditions, these signs warn travellers of unusual situations like work zones ahead, detours, lane closures, or traffic control people on the road. You should obey the instructions attentively as construction zones in most cases bring additional hazards.

WHITE :

Regulatory signs
The utilization of regulatory signs consists of the
implication or reinforcement of the laws regulating traffic. Regulations that apply at all times or within a predetermined window of time or place, either on streets or highways or a general regulatory sign that governs public behaviour

BLACK :

Lane control signs
The lane control signs consist of managing the flow of traffic on certain lanes by permitting or prohibiting access to them.

THE SHAPES OF ROAD SIGNS

Besides the colours, you can tell a lot about road signs by their shapes. They will give you your first piece of information. The shapes of road signs that are the most commonly found are **triangles, diamonds, rectangles, and circles.**

1/ The actions inside the circle are permitted:

2/ The actions shown inside the circle are not Allowed

3/ These shapes often reveal that a school zone or a crosswalk ahead

4/ This Sign Shows information or Instruction About Either Distance or Destination

5/ A Sign of a Regulatory Instruction Like speed limitation:

6/This sign reveal caution of a hazard ahead on the road

7/ This Sign reveals places for fuel or Food, lodging, or Assistance

8/ This Sign Inform You On a construction area or Temporary Work On the Road

9/ Reveals Lane control Ahead

REGULATORY SIGNS

The most prominent road signs are regulatory signs. The term "regulatory" is derived from the word "regulation," which refers to laws. And if it is law, it must be adhered to.

Regulatory signs unlike the other classified road signs come in various shapes. However, the commonly used colours in this specific classification are usually **red white, and black**.

Imperatively, drivers must have knowledge of these for the purposes of road tests to be successful either on the learner's or in on-road tests.

STOP SIGNS are eight-sided (octagonal shape) with a white border, and the word written on them is STOP. (Stop can be translated to Arret in French) and they stand for imperative stopping at the intersection where they are placed.

YIELD SIGNS are three-sided (Downside triangle), they have large red borders and the background is white. They signal to the driver that they must give way to oncoming traffic or pedestrians when entering the road.

SPEED LIMITATIONS/ TRAFFIC MOVEMENT SIGNS are four-sided (rectangular shape) with a black border and white background. They are often speed signs but can be about

slow movement in the traffic. That is been said that drivers who drive slowly should move over to the right lane so other drivers may pass for better traffic flow.

RAILWAY CROSSING SIGNS are shaped like an X with red borders and white background. Be cautious as you drive over a train track. *(See Page 19)*

SCHOOL ZONE SIGNS are five-sided (pentagon in shape) Most of these signs are in neon green. These signs indicate that you are coming to a school area, Which implies that you need to drive with a speed limit of 20-30 km/h *(See Page 19).*

PERMISSIVE SIGNS are square in shape with black border and the Background colour is green circle, and they provide drivers with information on actions and movements they are allowed to do on the road. For example, the displayed signs mean that PARKING is allowed and the double arrow indicates that it is valid for the entire block.

PROHIBITIVE SIGNS on the other hand, are square in shape with a black border, white Background and a red circle warn drivers about actions that are not allowed on the road, for example, the displayed sign means that you are not allowed to go straight on the intersection ahead.

LANE USAGE SIGNS

They are four-sided (rectangular shape) coloured white and black signs that indicate which lanes on a highway or freeway should be used for specific types of turns or movements.

These signs are typically placed above or to the side of the road and use arrows or other symbols to indicate the recommended lane usage, they are also correlated with road markings.

TRAFFIC DIRECTION LANE

Proceed in direction of the arrow only:

Two way traffic	Two way Left turn	Divider ahead keep right

Speed limit signs

The recommended maximum speed through the lane under normal conditions.

RESTRICTED USAGE LANE

In some urban centers, to improve the safety and flow of traffic, certain lanes have been reserved for specific uses, indicated by traffic signs. there are several types of restricted usage lanes that drivers should be aware of. These include:

Express Lanes: Express lanes, also known as toll lanes, are typically found on freeways. These lanes are reserved for drivers who pay a toll, or for vehicles with a certain number of passengers (carpool, vanpool). They are intended to provide a faster and more reliable trip for those willing to pay a toll.

Bus-only lanes: Bus-only lanes are designated lanes on highways and freeways that are reserved for buses only. These lanes are intended to improve the efficiency and reliability of bus service.

Bike lanes: Bike lanes are designated lanes on roads that are reserved for bicycles. They are intended to improve the safety and accessibility of biking as a mode of transportation.

Truck lanes: Some freeways have designated lanes for trucks, those lanes are intended to improve safety and mobility for truck drivers.

High-occupancy vehicle lanes commonly referred to as HOV lanes: also known as carpool lanes, are designated lanes on highways and freeways that are reserved for vehicles with a certain number of passengers. These lanes are intended to encourage carpooling and reduce traffic congestion.

HOV lanes are marked with a diamond symbol and are separated from regular lanes by a solid white line. The number of passengers required to use HOV lanes varies depending on the location and time of day. vehicles must have at least two or more occupants to use the HOV lane during rush hours,

CONSTRUCTION SIGNS

Construction signs are orange with a black stroke and the symbols or writings on them are black. Most of the time rectangular or diamond in shape. Their main role is to **warn you of potential hazards and obstructions** on the roadway, and they often indicate temporary conditions that may not be present at other times.

Construction signs are one part of a larger system that helps keep drivers safe in construction zones. Pylons, flaggers, flashing lights, signs, and even pilot vehicles may also be present to guide you through the construction zone safely.

They have reduced speed limits to ensure the safety of both drivers and construction workers.

Fines for speeding in construction zones are also higher than standard speeding fines.

 This sign notifies you of the presence of flaggers at a construction site, you are **required by law** to **follow their instructions**

 This sign indicates that **there are workers** on construction sites, thus be careful and reduce your speed

Pylons on construction zones are orange and black striped, you can see in construction areas most of the time diggers that are a characteristic of construction zones. Construction zones also can be surrounded by fences, which creates a distinct physical barrier between traffic and construction zones.

GUIDE SIGNS

Guide signs communicate important information that facilitates safe navigation, including information regarding **directional guidance, intersecting roads, desirable destination distance, and the location of services on the road**. They have a green background and display their message via text or logo. Here are three instances of guide signs commonly found on highways and expressways.

SCHOOL ZONES SIGNS

The first school sign gives you an advanced notice that there is a school in and around the area and if there are children present on the roadway, reduce your speed, and don't pass vehicles travelling in the same direction.

In Alberta, the school zone speed limit is generally **20-30 Km/hour** unless a road sign says otherwise.

Pay extra caution during specified hours when children are present. generally **between 8 am and 5 pm** during school days, and to posted signs, as the speed limit may be different depending on the location. Always obey traffic laws and be aware of your surroundings when driving in a school zone .

Passing in school zones can be incredibly dangerous. they are designated areas where children and families are crossing roads, walking to and from school, and playing. Passing in these zones increases the likelihood of accidents and children can be unpredictable.

RAILROAD CROSSING

One of the reasons why railway crossings are an important compound of the driving experience is because they present unique safety challenges, as they involve severe consequences and greater risks, due to the longer braking distance of rails and the fact that they may not necessarily keep a steady schedule.

You need to know also that **trains have always the right-of-way**. And that at night the risk of an incident multiplies as drivers don't have **a clear vision**. therefore, appropriate warning signs will be displayed to promote safety

ADVANCED WARNING SIGNS

Many railway crossings have warning signs that alert drivers beforehand that they are approaching a railway crossing. These signs are often accompanied by road markings. All railway crossings that intersect with roadways have advanced traffic control signs, signals, flashing lights, crossing gates, or even flaggers.

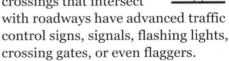

In the absence of signals at the railroad crossing, you should reduce your speed and be ready to stop if a train is seen or heard approaching. In the worst-case scenario, if you are stuck on a rail track and a train is on its way, leave the vehicle immediately

Under no circumstances should your vehicle come to a stop on a railroad track, and make sure to not cross a railway if there is traffic congestion or anything that will put you at risk

Note that even when the crossing gates are not down or the lights are not flashing, it is still necessary to stop, look both ways and listen for a train before crossing the tracks.

WARNING SIGNS

The cautionary or advisory signs are the second most frequently observed signs on the roadways. Typically, they are four-sided with a diamond or rectangular shape and a yellow background. The symbols and writings on them are black.

Hazard marker objects play a crucial role in alerting drivers to potential hazards and obstructions. They indicate which side to pass on and whether passing is permitted on the right or left.

CHANGING ROAD CONDITION

Hill   **Bumps**

Pavement ends   **Slippery when wet**

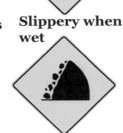

Dead End   **Falling rocks**

Chevron sign indicates a sharp bend in the road

Sharp turn Left   **Right turn curve**

Hazard marker objects near the road's edge are necessary to caution drivers about potential dangers

Left   Right

DIVIDED HIGHWAY SIGNS

Road curves right than left   **Winding road**

Divided highway begins   **Divided highway ends**

Road narrows both sides   **Narrow passage**

Crossroad   **The advisory speed limit**

PAVEMENT MARKINGS

Pavement markings work in tandem with traffic signs and stoplight signals to provide crucial details regarding the traffic flow and where you may and may not go to ensure everyone's safety.

Concrete patterns (straight or broken line) Different colours and numbers (white or yellow) (single or double) play a major role in separating lanes of traffic, displaying the change in roadways, identifying pedestrian movement, highlighting obstructions, and warning when it is unsafe to overtake, change lanes or make a U-turn.

Yellow line markings separate traffic moving in the opposite direction, marking the center of a roadway and on divided highways, they mark the left edge. On the other hand, **White lane markings** separate traffic moving in the same direction and mark the edge of a roadway.

A Solid line marking indicates restricted movement, which means that crossing the solid line to pass or change is prohibited.

Broken line marking means that crossing the broken line to pass or change lanes is permitted.

YELLOW LANE MARKING

A **broken yellow line** mark a passing zone, you may drive on the left lane to pass other vehicles, only when it is safe to do so.

Solid yellow lines, single or double to the left of your lane indicate that passing is risky and therefore **not allowed**.

A **solid yellow line along with a broken yellow line** means that passing is allowed for drivers who have the broken line on their side. Nevertheless, it is prohibited for the driver with the solid yellow line on their side to pass or turn.

WHITE LANE MARKINGS

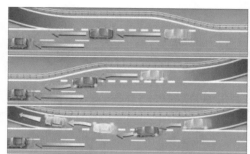

A solid white line in the middle of the road is used to separate traffic travelling in the same direction and indicates that crossing the line is not allowed, except in cases where it is necessary such as **avoiding an accident or a hazardous obstruction**.

It may also indicate the edge of the roadway and help drivers understand the limits of the road.

If you see **continuous lines** on your left-hand side, it usually means that the lane you are currently driving in is ending or diverging, and you will need to change lanes to continue on your intended route.

On the other hand, continuous lines on your right indicate that your lane will continue uninterrupted and you may stay in your current lane.

Broken or dashed white lines indicate that it is safe to cross the lines, as long as you do so when it is safe and the traffic is going in the same direction as you are.

A stop line is a single white line painted across the road. It indicates that you need to stop just before the line. If there is no stop line marked, you should still stop.

When transitioning **from a solid to a dashed** white line, means that you are permitted to change lanes once you have crossed over the dashed line

You may only go in the direction indicated by the arrow.

TWO WAY LEFT TURN MARKINGS

 Solid and broken yellow lines are also used for **center left turning lanes,** which are often located on main thoroughfares in the center of the road, allowing you to turn from a major road onto a minor road.

The center lane is for left turns only - it is not a passing lane. Make sure to position your vehicle correctly in the lane so as not to block traffic.

There is also a two-way left turn center lane, which means that traffic from both directions can use the lane for left turns. You do not need to worry about collisions because if a left-turning vehicle is coming from the opposite direction, it will be a fair distance away.

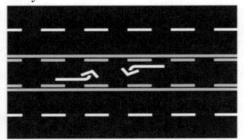

Two-way left turning center lane

RAILWAY CROSSING

 Trains always have the right-of-way. This is because trains require a significant distance to come to a stop and are less maneuverable.

Most railway crossings are marked with an X symbol and may also have electrical and mechanical warning devices such as flashing lights.

X markings indicate that you are coming to the railway crossing. If a train is approaching, you must stop and give the right of way to the train. Be sure to stop before the X marking to ensure your safety.

ACCESSIBLE PARKING VIA PERMIT ONLY

 As a holder of an accessible parking permit, it's essential that you always display your current permit on the dashboard or sun visor of the vehicle you are travelling in. This ensures that the permit number and expiry date are clearly visible to anyone who needs to see it.

The only person allowed to use the permit for parking is the individual whose name appears clearly. Using the permit for parking privileges without the permit holder present may result in severe consequences, including the suspension of the permit and a substantial penalty.

Hence, it's crucial to follow the rules related to accessible parking permits to ensure that they remain available to those who genuinely need them.

TRAFFIC ISLAND

Traffic islands are there to help traffic flow, separate lanes of traffic, and provide refuge for pedestrians.When you see yellow lines painted on an island, it means they are there to separate traffic in opposite directions. As a result, you should never drive on the island treat the yellow lines on the island as if they were solid lines, and stay on the right side of them at all times.

 A Traffic island's utility relies on it's positioning on the road, generally they have a traffic control advantages in the sense that they optimize traffic flow, in other cases they may be utilized to house infrastructure such as traffic lights or signs or to channel traffic onto a desired direction or as far as a form of traffic calming by narrowing the roadway or introducing curves.

DIAMOND LANE MARKINGS

Diamonds lanes are a restricted **lanes**, that's been said, only certain vehicles meeting the posted criteria on the sign are allowed to travel on those specific **lanes**. These criteria can be either related to the type of vehicle or certain times and dates in which they can use the lane in question usually in the rush hours.

Shared used lanes or **Sharrows** are used to alert motorists that bicyclists may occupy the travel lane. They can also help bicyclists maintain a safe lane position.

SYMBOLS

These symbols are utilized on the pavement to aid road users. They can also be used by themselves for the purpose of alerting the driver to guide or regulate the traffic. These markings may involve:

 Arrows: The movements of vehicles that are permitted in a particular lane are indicated by the arrows.

Railroad crossing road marking symbol: displayed in intersections prior to entering a railroad crossing

Facilities accessible for disabled individuals such as parking places, stairs, etc.

Diamond lanes indicate that the lane is reserved for specific types of vehicles

Sharrows This symbol marks a lane shared by motorists and bicyclists.

Your driving privilege may be suspended or revoked for a variety of reasons. One of them **is accumulating points on your driving record**. Perhaps you're already familiar with this (dreaded) point system, which is designed to penalize drivers for traffic violations and encourage safety on the road. Each traffic violation is assigned a specific number of points in this case, and drivers who accumulate too many of these within a given timeframe may face dire consequences such as a license suspension or sky-high insurance rates.

On your driving record, you never **"lose"** your demerit points. Initially, you start with zero points. Then, when you are convicted of violating a particular traffic law, you begin to gain these points.

LAW ENFORCEMENT STOP

there is nothing to worry about in case you were asked to pull over by a law enforcement officer as it is a normal procedure and doesn't necessarily mean that you did infract the law.

During a Law enforcement stop by the Police make sure that the police officer acknowledges that you have noticed him and switch on your right-turn signal. Even if you're in a restricted usage lane, go entirely to the right shoulder. When feasible, come to a full stop in a very well-lit place.

A. Pull over to a safe location as soon as possible. Turn on your hazard lights to indicate that you are complying.
B. Unless the police tell you otherwise, stay in your vehicle.
C. Sudden movements, especially reaching into pockets or the glove compartment, can be perceived as a threat. Inform the officer of your actions before making any moves.
D. Make sure **your hands and the hands of all passengers are visible.** They can be on your wheel or dashboard for example.

When a car is stopped by law enforcement, the driver must present a **valid driver's license, evidence of insurance coverage, and vehicle registration.**

Motorists should always avoid interrupting or intervening with the police officer's responsibilities during the traffic stop and act as courteously as possible.

You should know also that law enforcement **has the legal authority** to search your car under certain conditions without your agreement.

25

DEMERIT POINTS

Demerit points apply to licence holders who infract the law. That being said, whenever you are convicted of violating any of Alberta's driving laws certain demerit points will be added to your driving licence record.

A conviction of an offence can be considered valid by paying the fine on your ticket, appearing in a court where you are found guilty or failing to appear in court while you are found guilty in absence.

Driving a motor vehicle **while your driver's license is suspended** can result in **jail time, fines, or both.**

LIST OF DEMERIT POINTS

You will get 7 demerit points for: Failing to stay at the scene where the accident has taken place

You will receive 6 demerit points for: Irresponsible driving and driving with a speed that is 50 km/hr over the posted or statutory speed limit. Not driving carefully Involved in racing and not stopping for a school bus.

You will receive 5 demerit points for: Not stopping and giving the required information to a police officer. Not stopping at an uncontrolled railway crossing, And in a railway crossing if a vehicle is carrying gas, flammable liquids, or explosives.

You will receive 4 demerit points for: Driving with a speed that is 30 km/hr over the specified speed limit of up to 50 km/hr. Following closely and

not yielding the right of way at a pedestrian crossing.

You will receive 3 demerit points for: Driving with a speed that is 16 km/hr over the specified speed limit of up to 30 km/hr. Not reporting a collision, Failing to stop at an intersection controlled by a stop sign or a stoplight, Taking the wrong direction on a one-way highway, Impeding passing vehicle and Improper passing, Driving to the left of the yellow line / Driving left of center on unmarked two-way, Doing stunts on the road.

PENALTIES FOR DEMERIT POINTS

If you are a Graduated Driver's Licence (GDL) driver here is the breakdown; If your demerit point total is between **four and seven** within two years, a cautionary notice will be sent to you. However, if you accumulate eight or more demerit points during that same two-year period, you will get the first licence **suspension for 1 month.**

For the second demerit point suspension within a year, your licence will be **suspended for 3 months.** The third and subsequent suspensions within a period **of 2 years involve a 6-month suspension**

The drivers who have full (non-GDL) licences get a cautionary notice with regards to their driving record if they accumulate a total **(8 to 14 points)** in a span **of two years.**

Your licence will get suspended for **a period of 30 days** in case you get **15 demerit points** or more within the period of two years. For a second demerit point suspension you will face a **3-month driver's privilege suspension**. You will lose your driving license for a **period of 6 months** in case you receive a third or subsequent demerit point suspension **within two years**.

When your suspension ends, your abstract or driving record will be reinstated with **7 demerit points (3 for GDL Drivers)** that will remain on your record for 2 years.

You can request **a review of the demerit points** to make sure that they aren't assigned to you by error, by submitting a plea to the driving fitness and monitoring. Nevertheless, you cannot appeal a demerit points.

YOUR DUTY AFTER A COLLISION

Unless you're directly involved or emergency aid has not yet arrived, **never stop at an auto accident** site as you can potentially block traffic or cause further hazards/potential accidents on the roadway.

It's certainly no secret that being involved in a vehicle crash resulting in bodily injury, property damage, or (tragically) death is an overwhelmingly stressful experience.

Nevertheless, you'll need to pull up your bootstraps to **provide information** and **render aid** as necessary: trying your absolute best to remain calm and follow the proper procedures, which can go a long way toward keeping everyone around safe.

You'll also need to **exchange information** for the vehicle(s), witness(es), and driver(s) involved—including **names, addresses, phone numbers, license plate numbers, and driver's license/insurance information.**

Immediately call 911 (especially if someone is hurt) or local law enforcement in the aftermath of a crash, and **turn on your hazard lights**. Take **photos or manually sketch** the scene if necessary, showing vehicle crash locations and any other pertinent details. A law enforcement officer should complete a written report, especially (of course) if the crash involves suspicion of DUI and/or results in death, injury, or property damage.

if you experience **an accident with an unattended vehicle** (or any other type of property, for that matter), you're obligated to make every possible attempt to locate the owner and notify law enforcement about the incident. **Unable to locate** the property owner? **Leave a note** behind that includes your name, contact information, and the date/time of the accident.

According to Alberta province laws, All collisions must be reported to the police or local law enforcement if anyone has been injured or killed, or if the overall damage **exceeds $2,000**. If police are called to the scene, all drivers must remain.

Finally, If someone is injured, apply first aid if you're trained to do so; **never attempt to move or transfer an injured person**, however, to avoid aggravating a potential neck, spinal, or other injury. If the accident involves an injured motorcyclist or bicycle rider, **avoid removing his or her helmet** for the same reason.

FENDER BENDER
MOVE VEHICLES FROM TRAVEL LANES Generally and most especially when a " **fender bender**" in other words minimal damage accident (no injuries, minor vehicle damage) sign is displayed, all parties involved in the crash are required **to move their vehicles to the shoulder of the road** after taking pictures or drawing the position of their vehicles in the scene of the accident.

YOUR FINANCIAL RESPONSIBILITY

As liability insurance also known as **Third-party liability.** is mandatory for all motor vehicle owners, all vehicles registered in Alberta must have this coverage to pay for any damages or injuries that occur in the event of an auto accident.

Keep in mind, however, that this coverage only extends to costs incurred by the other party in this case—rather than your expenses. That's precisely why experts recommend seeking out higher liability limits or additional insurance options (e.g., collision and comprehensive coverage) to fully protect yourself financially should you land in this unfortunate situation.

There are two parts to this coverage :

1/ Bodily injury liability: This provides coverage against lawsuits for medical expenses, pain, suffering, funeral costs, lost wages or other special damages after an auto accident.

2/ Property damage liability: This provides coverage against lawsuits arising from damaged property if you have a registered and plated vehicle that is driving down a roadway in Alberta

These two coverages are mandatory. You are required to have a **minimum limit of $200.000** in third-party liability.

Evidence of financial responsibility, meanwhile, is required in the wake of an accident or law enforcement stop as proof that a motor vehicle owner has the means to pay for any damages/injuries that may have occurred. The most common form of said evidence? A liability insurance policy with at least the minimum required amount OR **standard proof** of liability insurance such as a certificate.

SEATBELT LAWS

In Alberta, it is mandatory for drivers and passengers to be securely fastened inside a vehicle using a seat belt or a government-approved child safety seat attached either by a seat belt or anchor system. Failure to do so can result in a **fine for passengers 16 years and older** who are not properly secured.

As the driver, **you are responsible** for ensuring that **all passengers under the age of 16 are properly secured**, and failure to do so can result in a fine for you.

All child safety seats used in Canada must have a label that confirms compliance **with Canada Motor Vehicle Safety Standard 213**, which should not be ignored. It is essential to avoid using a child safety seat intended for use in countries other than Canada.

If the child is **under the age of six and weighs less than 18 kilograms (40 pounds),** they must be secured in a child safety seat installed following the manufacturer's instructions for both the vehicle and the child safety seat.

You are responsible as a driver for fastening your seatbelt and ensuring that

- Everyone has their own, properly working seatbelt.
- **Under the age of 16** passengers are **wearing** their seatbelts properly.
- **Children** are secured in an **appropriate** child **car seat** or **booster seat** that fits their **height, weight and/or age.**

it is required that all children ride in a rear-facing infant seat or rear-facing convertible seat until they reach the recommended weight specified by the manufacturer to switch to a forward-facing safety seat.

Forward-facing child safety seats are designed for children weighing **between 10 to 18 kilograms (22 to 40 pounds)**. Both newer vehicles and child safety seats are equipped with the universal anchor system or UAS/LATCH.

Children who weigh **more than 18 kilograms (40 pounds)** must use an approved **booster seat** before using only the vehicle's seat belt without a booster seat. It is crucial to use the seat according to the manufacturer's instructions.

Finding the perfect child seat requires careful consideration of several factors, including the right fit for your child, car, and consistent usage. Thus, read the instructions manual for the safest seats.

IMPAIRED DRIVING

Impaired driving infractions include driving without regard to your blood alcohol levels or exceeding the legal limits (**80 milligrams of alcohol in 100 millilitres of blood or 0.08**) drug consumption, a combination of both, refusing to obey police officer instructions to give a breath or blood sample, causing bodily damage or death and driving while your licence is suspended or disqualified for an impaired driving reason.

All of the critical abilities required to drive safely are impaired by alcohol, including judgment, reaction time, vision, and focus. Driving under the influence of alcohol or any drug that can impair your driving ability is illegal in Alberta.

This is valid for many prescription treatments as well as over-the-counter cold and allergy remedies. This is why the province has a system in place called **the Immediate Roadside Sanctions (IRS) Program** that regulates violations of the law.

If you are found driving or in real physical control of a vehicle while under the influence of alcoholic beverages, controlled substances, prescriptions, or over-the-counter medications that can impair your driving ability, **you can be charged with DUI.**

In fact, **IRS WARN program** applies in situations where a law enforcement officer has logical reasons to believe that a driver has operated a vehicle under the influence of alcohol or a drug.

ZERO Novice program explicitly indicates that there is no tolerance for alcohol and drug consumption for the class 7 learner's licence or class 5 GDL licence drivers.

An ignition interlock device can be attached to the vehicle with a built-in breathalyzer to prevent the engine from starting if the driver is convicted of a DUI as a precautionary mechanism.

It is a common misconception that consuming water, coffee, or engaging in physical exercise can rapidly reduce blood alcohol content. In reality, these methods do not expedite the body's ability to metabolize alcohol.

The question is, is there any method that lowers your BAC after drinking? The answer is, that the only effective way to lower **BAC is to allow sufficient time** for the liver to process and eliminate alcohol from the bloodstream.

Not only that! The liver metabolizes alcohol **at a relatively constant rate,** and attempting to accelerate this process through hydration or exercise **does not** alter the body's natural detoxification timeline.

DISTRACTED DRIVING

Distracted driving is a very dangerous habit that endangers not only you and your passengers but also other vulnerable road users such as bicycles and pedestrians. Reading, writing, or sending messages on a hand-held gadget like a cell phone is prohibited by law. Other common distractions include:

- Using a cell phone.
- Looking at something, someone, or something inside or outside the car.
- reaching for something.
- unattended pets.
- Grooming.

It is prompted not to reply to calls on your cell phone. Unless you **pull off** the road **and park** your vehicle, by then you can use your phone to answer your calls or text back.

For your best interest, familiarize yourself with all the safety and use features of any in-car electronics, including your car play or cockpit features before you start driving and it is preferable to schedule your favourite radio stations or music you often listen to well in advance. Additionally, steer clear of engaging in complex or candid conversations with other passengers in the car

Driving **while fatigued** might also be just as risky as distracted driving. since:

- Your thinking and reaction time will be slowed down.
- Your judgment and eyesight can be affected.
- and/or you may be nodding or falling completely asleep.

BRAKING SYSTEM

ABS

 Anti-lock brakes (ABS) prevent wheel lock-up, especially if the steer tires are in an emergency braking situation. essentially they will release the brakes The way that you would know that your vehicle has ABS brakes or if they are still working is by checking your dashboard, the ABS lights should come on momentarily.

The ABS brakes don't stop you at short distances, they are effective for strong brakes and on slippery roads as well so when there is snow or rain outside, ABS brakes will engage much more quickly and are prone to doing that on slippery conditions a lot more than on dry pavement.

Push hard, hold the brake pedal to the full capacity and look in the direction you want the vehicle to go to. After the execution, you can hear a noise and the shutter (grinding noise and you can feel the vehicle pulsating) and that is the ABS brake engaging.

LOWER GEAR BRAKING

```
USE LOWER
   GEAR
─────────────
RÉTROGRADEZ
```
The brakes will deteriorate if you are **repeatedly** pressing on the brakes to slow down when **descending a steep hill**. Release the gas and **change into a lower gear instead**. This will provide **engine braking**, which will cause the car to slow down. The engine braking effect **increases** with **lower gearing**.

ALBERTA SPEED LAWS

In the Province of Alberta, speed limits are set by the Ministry of Transportation and enforced by law enforcement authorities. The speed limits are mostly displayed via signs along the roadway and are based on the type of road, vehicle, weather conditions and the surrounding area.

THE 4 MAJOR SPEED LAWS

MAXIMUM 70 **The maximum speed law** basically means you are not allowed to exceed the speed limit posted on a road sign. The following signs suggest different speed limits depending on the **location, type of vehicle, or time**.

The basic speed law is the most common of all and states that you should not exceed a safe speed on a roadway **based on weather and road conditions**. That being said, Speed restrictions indicate the fastest possible speed under ideal conditions, you must alter your driving speed in response to weather, road, and traffic circumstances. During rainy weather, for example, you should drive slower than the posted speed limit. The safest speed is one that gives you entire control of your car and allows you to avoid crashes.

The statutory or prima facie speed law mandates a statutory speed limit in areas where speed signs may not be posted, nevertheless, they should be known and followed by default.

The following are statutory speed limits :

- **30 to 50 km/h** on city roads
- **60 to 80 km/h** on rural highways and country roads
- **90 km/h** on Trans-Canada
- **100 to 110 km/h** in freeways
- **30 to 40 km/h** in school zones

SPEED LIMIT 65 MINIMUM 40 There is a law known as **the "Minimum Speed Regulation"** that requires drivers not to drive at a speed that is slower and excessively prudent, therefore it can impede, interrupt, or even block the normal flow of traffic.

When driving below the posted speed limit in multilane roads you must drive **in the right-hand lane.** Failure to follow this law can result in a traffic citation and fines.

Vice versa, the leftmost lane is dedicated to vehicles who want to **drive faster or pass** other vehicles while respecting the posted or statutory speed limit.

The Difference between these two Speed signs

Mandatory   *Advisory*

RIGHT-OF-WAY RULES

There is no denying the fact that there are high chances of collisions occurring at intersections, as we don't know who must move and who needs to yield. **The right-of-way** is a crucial rule that defines when and who should proceed first in such situations.

Rules of the road are generally established via signs, signals, and the location of your vehicle regarding other vehicles. Thus, the right-of-way rule requires one person to yield and allow the other to proceed following their position on the road.

Despite having the complete edge of the situation, you are still expected to demonstrate a responsible attitude by doing whatever it takes to avoid accidents. **A golden rule** is that the right-of-way is **always yielded, never seized**.

Directions and instructions **from a police officer** in an intersection or elsewhere **take precedence** over traffic signs or signals.

Throughout this chapter, we will explore the rules of right-of-way in **different scenarios**, including at intersections, during merging, and at roundabouts.

Driving at intersections is a very important component of the driving experience, this is because Intersections witness **a higher**

frequency of accidents than any other location, and it's the one place where you're most likely to encounter and cross paths with vulnerable road users such as pedestrians, cyclists, motorcycle riders, scooters, and skaters.

INTERSECTIONS

An intersection is a point or area of the roadway where **two or more** roads converge, diverge, meet, or cross paths. It can take the form of a crossroad, commonly known as a four-way intersection or a T-junction or Y-junction in the case of three-way intersections, and vehicles need to interact with each other by stopping, yielding, or proceeding based on established traffic rules.

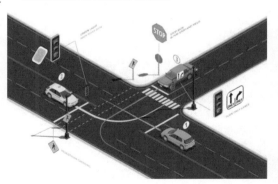

There are two types of intersections, the first one is a **controlled** intersection, meaning that it relies on traffic control signs and signals to control traffic flow. The second type is **uncontrolled** or blind intersections that use right-of-way rules for the same goal.

When a vehicle is about to turn on a roadway, common signs include **using signals, slowing down, and hesitating.** Pedestrians on the roadside may communicate to drivers that they intend to cross the street via eye contact or other nonverbal communication actions.

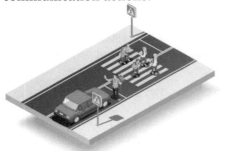

Traffic flow on the road

Blocking an intersection is generally considered to be a traffic violation as it can lead to traffic congestion and delays. In most jurisdictions in North America, it is illegal for a driver to enter an intersection if they **cannot clear it** before the traffic signal turns red or if traffic ahead of them stops.

The aim is to ensure that traffic can continue to flow smoothly and safely to prevent gridlock and to avoid compromising public safety, as such a situation can hinder the response time of emergency vehicles.

When an **emergency vehicle** is on its way and you're in an intersection hearing the siren of an emergency vehicle approaching, **never stop in an intersection, proceed through first**. then, pull over to the right at the earliest safe opportunity and come to a stop. Avoid making **sudden maneuvers** that could create further confusion or contribute to aggravating

the traffic congestion, and make sure your intentions are clear and communicated priorly via vehicle signals, hand signals, eye contact, or even verbal communication if the situation requires so.

When approaching an intersection, it is crucial to not only scan ahead but also check for cross traffic and pedestrians. Misjudging pedestrians can cause delays in the intersection and **lead to blockage as well**. Therefore, it's important to drive slowly, stay calm, and be able to interpret traffic patterns and predict the actions of other drivers.

CONTROLLED INTERSECTIONS

Controlled intersections **rely on stop signs, yield signs, and traffic lights** for traffic management.

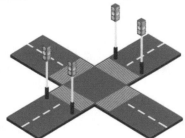

Controlled by a stoplight

In this case, the right of way is determined by the stoplight. If you encounter a **stoplight**, and the light is currently green, you should be aware that it may turn yellow soon. If you're unable to stop safely because you are already too close to the intersection, you should **proceed through** with extreme caution.

If the light turns red while you are at the intersection, **stay calm and wait until there is sufficient space** to proceed in the direction you want to move to, but only when you are completely sure of completing the maneuver safely.

If you **plan to turn left** and face a long line of oncoming traffic, here's what you should do. When the light eventually turns green for both directions, position your front steering tires on the front crosswalk line and wait. Anticipate a gap in traffic, and after the opposite direction traffic clears, check your shoulder and make the left turn.

Controlled by a stop sign: Bring your vehicle to a complete stop, and if you can't see the cross-traffic or the intersection, then creep forward.

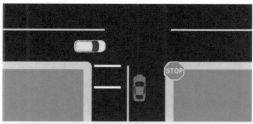

Note that there should be enough room (10 feet) for the pedestrians to walk by easily.

Two-way Stop sign intersection

You will most likely find a two-way stop sign intersection in the residential areas and there is going to be a major thoroughfare through those areas and all the minor roads must have stop signs. A two-way stop sign intersection is exactly as it sounds: in a four-way intersection, **two corners have** stop signs, while the other **two do not.** And it has different rules compared to the 3/4 way stop sign intersections. More particularly, the general rule of first to stop first to go **does not** apply here:

Hereby, the rules in this setup:

A. **Pedestrians first**
B. After that **major roads** have the right of way over **minor roads (or** the cross traffic who aren't controlled by a stop sign)
C. Straight through traffic over turning traffic
D. **Right-turning** over left-turning

Given this set-up, If two vehicles arrive and **they don't cross paths**, they can go **simultaneously**, for example, if they are both going straight from opposite directions or if one is going straight and the other is turning right.

Stop completely at the indicated stop line. Wait until pedestrians can safely pass and the way is clear proceed

Do not cross a marked crosswalk when coming to a stop.

If there is no crosswalk or a stop line, stop before the intersecting roads at a distance of 10 feet.

Three and four way Stops intersections:

At a 3-way stop, also known as a T-intersection, all points of entry to the intersection must come to a complete stop before proceeding through. This rule applies not only to 3-way intersections but also to 4-way intersections and those with more points of entry.

When approaching a busy 4-way intersection, there are a few key pieces of information to keep in mind. Most 4-way stops have clearly marked stop lines, making it easy to know where to stop. In addition, because these intersections tend to be heavily trafficked, there are typically designated crosswalks for pedestrians.

Unlike a 2-way stop intersection, the right-of-way rule at a 3 and 4 ways stop is as follows *(See point B):*

A. Pedestrians first
B. **followed by the first vehicle to arrive or stop, first to go.**
C. If two or more vehicles arrive simultaneously, the vehicle **on the right** has the right-of-way.
D. When it comes to turning, vehicles **going straight** have priority over turning vehicles.
E. If two vehicles are turning, the one making **a right turn** has the right-of-way over the one making a left turn.

"Courtesy corners" refer to intersections with stop signs on all corners. All four approaching vehicles arrive at the same time, this implies that there **is a car to everyone's right**, meaning that this situation can cause confusion. In this case, either you or another driver should take the initiative by slightly moving forward and observing the other vehicle's reaction. If they give you the courtesy by letting you proceed, then the right-over-left vehicle rule applies to the rest of the vehicles at the intersection.

Controlled by a yield sign:

Yield signs mandate that drivers at intersections give the right of way to other road users already present, or alert drivers to approaching hazards.

When approaching a junction with a yield sign, drivers must come to a full stop and wait for any pedestrians or vehicles in the intersection to clear before proceeding. Yield signs are not commonly found in residential areas but are instead utilized in areas with lighter traffic flow and reduced collision risks.

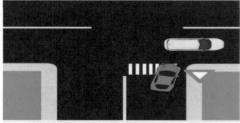

The right defensive position is to creep to the intersection to have a clear vision and to drive at a speed that permits you to stop with ease to prevent collisions.

UNCONTROLLED INTERSECTIONS

Uncontrolled or blind intersections are omnipresent in the quiet/residential areas where there is less volume of traffic. They can also be found in some industrial or rural zones. due to their unique nature, uncontrolled intersections have no traffic control signals or signs. You should scan the intersection very concisely to see if the other paths don't have any signs or lights.

The right-of-way rules in uncontrolled intersections **are exactly the same as in four-way** stop intersections:

In case you have reached an uncontrolled junction at the same time, the vehicle **that reached first** has the right of way over the vehicle arriving last.

If two vehicles arrive at the same time, the driver on the left must always yield to **the driver on the right**. However, the driver on the right must remain attentive to avoid any potential collisions.

Following traffic blindly at an intersection can be a dangerous habit. This can lead to an obstructed view by a large vehicle, truck, or commercial vehicle. Also, it may result in running a red light, causing potential accidents with cross traffic.

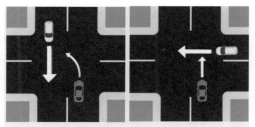

The blue car needs to yield to the **white car** in this case

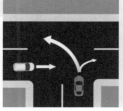

The white car needs to yield to the **Blue car** in case of both paths in this T shaped intersection

Be extremely cautious in this situation as the drivers that are going straight through (white) make the assumption that they do have the right of way incorrectly.

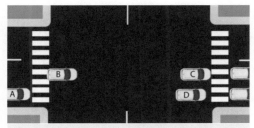

In this case, **A** is in the correct position. **B** has blocked the crosswalk. However, the **C** & **D** vehicles have used poor judgment

At pedestrian crossings and school crossings with a crosswalk, cede the right-of-way and wait for pedestrians to cross the road.

ROUNDABOUTS

Roundabouts are circular forms of intersections, with vehicles travelling around a central island, they are specifically designed to enhance the safety and flow of traffic. And because vehicles can flow continuously through a roundabout, there are several benefits to that:

Firstly, there is often **less congestion and shorter delays** compared to normal intersections.

Secondly, **accidents** that do occur in roundabouts tend to be **less severe**, as vehicles are typically travelling at lower speeds and the circular design promotes more glancing blows rather than direct collisions.

And finally, **they can be adapted to various traffic conditions** and can accommodate different road users, including pedestrians and cyclists by relying on pedestrian crosswalks with refuge islands.

Vehicles that enter the roundabout should **yield to the traffic already in it.** In North America, traffic in roundabouts travels in a **counterclockwise direction.**

Nevertheless, in countries like the UK and Australia where they drive on the left side of the road traffic will flow in a clockwise direction, so be aware of that.

To navigate a roundabout safely and effectively, the recommended speed at the roundabout is **20 to 30 Km/h.**

When exiting a roundabout, it's important to **signal your intention** to other drivers in advance to prevent accidents. For instance, if you are exiting from the left lane or making a U-turn, use your left turn signal to indicate your intention of turning left or making a U-turn.

Approach the exit with a reduced speed, ensuring you yield to any pedestrians in the crosswalk and **give priority to vehicles already within the roundabout**. Maintain a consistent speed as you navigate the exit curve. Always wait for a safe gap before merging into the next lane or onto the connecting road.

If you drive in a **multi-lane roundabout** you need to think of it as a conventional intersection. This means that every vehicle should travel in the appropriate lane based on its destination. To add that riders of motorcycles and bikes are entitled to use a full traffic lane.

More precisely, if you are travelling in **the right-hand lane**, your intention should be to make a **right turn or proceed straight through** the roundabout. Conversely, if you plan to make a U-turn or exit on the left, you should be in the left-hand lane.

Always be prepared to yield to vehicles **turning or exiting in front of you** from the inside as they have the right of way.

In a multi-lane roundabout, **do not overtake or attempt to overtake** because it can be a very dangerous maneuver. and only change lanes if road markings permit this action. Keep in mind that **predictability** is a key element when it comes to safety in roundabouts or intersections in general.

U- TURNS

U-turns are permitted only when they pose no danger to other road users. a common scenario that can make U-turns hazardous is executing them in locations **with limited visibility**, resulting in restrictions on such maneuvers.

These prohibited scenarios include: near the crest of hills or curves, interstate highways, busy business districts, whenever a no U-turn sign or signal is displayed, in the presence of solid white or yellow pavement marking on your side of the roadway, in an intersection controlled by a police officer, or any other situation where you or other motorists cannot see **500 feet away.**

When U-turns are allowed, visibility is clear but the road is narrow, you should perform a **3-point U-turn.**

If you happen to **miss your exit** on a freeway or highway, **never attempt to stop, back up, or make a U-turn.**

Here is how you can execute a 3 point U-turn:

A. Move as far right as possible, check traffic carefully, then use your left turn signal, Rotate the steering wheel to the left, and proceed forward at a slow pace.
B. Come to a halt at the curb or edge of the roadway. Transition to reverse, turn the wheels sharply to the right, verify traffic, and reverse your vehicle
C. By then, lightly adjust your steering wheel to the direction where you aim to go

MERGING LANES

Changing lanes is a very important component of defensive driving. Understand that when you move from one marked lane to another, you are required to give the right of way to the vehicles that are **already in that particular lane.** This applies to all situations, including when you are merging into a freeway.

To switch lanes safely, you must use your vehicle's signals to indicate your intention to change lanes and only make the move when there is a safe gap in the traffic.

Before accessing a highway or freeway, check for cross traffic and turn onto the acceleration lane. You are not considered to be on the acceleration lane until you pass the continuity lines.

Zip merging is when 2 lanes of traffic merge into one, on a road where there is no road marking, giving the right of way to any vehicle which has any part of its vehicle ahead of yours.

When merging back into traffic **after an emergency stop,** proceed with caution and observe your surroundings. Before attempting to merge, check your mirrors, and blind spots, and scan the road for any oncoming vehicles. Always signal your intention to merge by using your turn signal.

Tailgating means driving too closely to the vehicle in front, therefore it is an extremely dangerous behaviour on the road. When a driver tailgates, they leave little to no space to react in case the vehicle in front suddenly brakes or swerves. This greatly increases the risk of rear-ending the vehicle in front, which can result in serious injuries or even fatalities. Tailgating is also a traffic infraction, prohibited in all North American jurisdictions, and can result in hefty penalties and demerit points.

LANE MANAGEMENT

A key element to ensuring safety at intersections **is proper lane positioning** before making a turn. Being positioned in the correct lane well before entering an intersection allows for smooth and predictable traffic flow, and reduces the likelihood of last-minute maneuvers. This means that you should use the leftmost lane when making a left turn or U-turn, the middle lanes when going straight through, and the rightmost lane when turning right.

Pay attention to these lane control signs as they indicate **the direction specific lanes should follow**

For brand-new drivers, when and how to perform a shoulder check may pose a challenge, first of all, shoulder checks are an essential way to look for vehicles coming from behind and to check **for blind spots** while changing lanes, making a turn, or merging with existing traffic roadway, the technic is simple, quickly glance over your shoulder while having a safe following distance.

One of the most important rules of driving is to **never change lanes in an intersection.** This is because making sudden turns through an intersection or roundabout (which is also considered an intersection) makes you unpredictable and goes against safe driving practices. Even if there is no legislation presented for it, make sure to never change lanes in an intersection, as it significantly increases the chance of being involved in a risky situation.

When driving on **high-speed roads** such as interstates or freeways, you are required to use **the rightmost lane** in case you want to travel **slower than the flow of traffic**, and vice versa, if you decide to drive **faster,** but never above the posted or statutory speed limit, **the leftmost lane** is dedicated to that.

40

Numerous road users utilize Alberta's roadways, including pedestrians, motorcyclists, cyclists, large trucks, buses, and agricultural equipment. This means that each of them requires specific precautionary measures for the safety and comfort of all.

SHARING THE ROAD WITH OTHER ROAD USERS

PEDESTRIANS :

When it comes to crosswalks or intersections, pedestrians **have the right-of-way first at all times**.

Controlled intersections via a traffic light require pedestrians to give way when the light is green. Nevertheless, drivers need to always be cautious and give the way even if the light is green if a pedestrian is nonchalant about traffic rules, or if the light turned green while the pedestrian is on his way to complete the crosswalk.

A Right turn on red requires the driver **to stop**, check for traffic left and right, give way to pedestrians, and allow them ample time to cross.

Another **key element** to pedestrian safety is **eye contact** between both the pedestrian and the vehicle.

As a driver, it is important to know that stopping on the pedestrian crosswalk **is strictly illegal** as it forces pedestrians to walk around your vehicle out into moving traffic. Which puts their life in danger and makes them less visible for oncoming traffic.

Pay attention to pedestrians **at the edge of the crosswalk** getting ready to enter or from the other side of the street crossing. You still need to slow down and stop for pedestrians in the opposite direction of traffic.

When driving in residential areas or school zones, keep in mind that **children and youngsters are unpredictable and they** might **follow a ball** that is bouncing into the road. Use the same caution and consideration when a pedestrian is elderly or disabled, as they need more time to cross the street.

When nearing a **stationary vehicle** from the rear, reduce your speed and refrain from overtaking until you are certain there are no pedestrians in front.

Reminder: **Blind** or **visually impaired** pedestrians can use a **white cane** or a **guiding dog** to help them cross intersections.

BICYCLISTS

With the pleasant weather, the influx of bicycles and cyclists is inevitable and not all cyclists opt for helmets or reflective gear, making them potentially harder to notice. however, you should be on the lookout for those vulnerable road users and give them enough room so they can operate safely on the road.

As a vehicle driver, you need to understand well that not all bicyclists or riders have **the same skill level.** Therefore, some of them might be unpredictable.

In Alberta, **a 1-metre minimum passing** distance is required between vehicles and bicyclists.

Indeed, bicyclists are legal drivers with laws and regulations established for their use. Sharing the road with them means mutual respect which can be promoted by public information.

Follow the instructions below:

A. Yield to bicycles when turning.
B. Always give bicyclists more passing room in adverse weather
C. Make a visual check for bikes by checking mirrors and using shoulder checks before you enter or leave any lane of traffic.
D. Reduce your speed when passing bikes when the road is narrow.
E. Don't use your horn at bicyclists it can cause them to swerve into traffic or off the road.

MOTORCYCLISTS

Because of their dimensions, motorcycles can be hard to see or can hide in your blind spots, especially at night, in bad weather, or heavy traffic. They are also more prone to injury in a collision because they are less guarded.

You need also to allow **at least four to five seconds** of **following distance** when you are behind a motorcycle. Be cautious motorcycles are closer than they seem. And because of their smaller size, they may be harder to spot on your blind spots. And, same as cars, motorcycles are allowed **an entire lane**.

When motorbikes are slowing down they may use their throttle instead of their brake, so you may **not see the brake lights.** You need also to know that road conditions affect their driving differently such as uneven pavement and slippery roads.

Driving a quiet vehicle: Operators hybrid and electric cars should be aware that persons with low eyesight often depend on the sounds of an engine before approaching an intersection. Because a hybrid or electric car produces little or no perceptible noise while slowing or stopping.

COMMERCIAL VEHICLES

Driving safely in the presence of large commercial vehicles and eventually avoiding collision is the product of being familiar with their physical capabilities and maneuvers. Large commercial vehicles are designated to transport cargo and are not as maneuverable as passenger vehicles.

Large trucks have **longer stopping distances,** they take more space for turns and they weigh more. They also have **wider blind spots** to which your vehicle can get lost, the blind spots or no zone areas are: **directly in front, directly behind, and along each side**.

You need to be careful of all large heavy vehicles **that are turning**, they cannot see cars directly behind or beside them, and they may need to **use multiple lanes** to navigate turns safely. Never linger alongside a truck while passing, try to escape by passing the truck, or if it's not possible back off. pass or overtake a truck with care.

Try not to pass or overtake a truck on the left-hand side, this is because a truck blind spot on the left runs down the left of the trailer and extends out three lanes. for all turning vehicles the rear wheels follow a shorter path than the front wheels. Therefore, truck drivers frequently need to make wide turns when executing a right or left maneuver.

Ensure you can see the driver in their **side mirrors**; if you can't, they likely can't see you.

Always give room for doubt, if you think the truck is turning right wait a second and check the turning signals again the driver may be turning left. Also, avoid passing a turning truck or bus on the right, as they make wide turns that can pose a risk to vehicles on their right side.

Large commercial vehicles need a **significantly larger braking distance** than regular vehicles. When overtaking a huge vehicle, avoid getting in front of it. This is not only impolite, but it is also hazardous since it increases the safe distance required for huge cars to brake in time.

FLASHING LIGHTS SCHOOL BUS

When a stopped school bus has its red or amber lights flashing, **stop** regardless of being behind the bus or approaching it from the front. Considering that the bus is in front of you, stop at a **safe distance** to allow children to leave and cross the road ahead.

For those approaching it from behind, ensure that you stop at a safe distance and wait until the bus has moved or its lights stopped flashing before continuing your journey. Only traffic coming from the rear must stop if a **median strip** is separating the road.

A stop sign arm is used on the driver's side of school buses. This arm extends out once the red lights start to flash, and it resembles a typical stop sign. **Failing to do so** is very unlawful. you risk receiving a hefty fine and demerit points.

THE TWO-SECONDS RULE

Maintaining a safe gap between vehicles while driving is critical to prevent rear-end collisions. As it is known, tailgating or following too closely is an infraction of the law and can lead to rear-end collisions.

The Two-seconds rule guides drivers to maintain a safe while driving. It suggests that you should keep a gap of at **least 2 seconds**, to allow for a safe stopping distance in case of sudden braking or emergencies.

This rule is subject to change depending on road conditions, weather, and traffic density. the more there is time for a reaction

ENTERING A HIGHWAY

All entrances to limited access highways are comprised of three essential parts, **namely an entrance ramp, an acceleration lane, and a merging area.**

At the entrance ramp, you should start looking for an opening and signal your intention to merge onto the highway.

As the ramp straightens into the acceleration lane, increase your speed and adjust it accordingly to merge into traffic when you reach the end of the acceleration lane. Once you are in the merging area, make sure to yield the right-of-way to traffic on the highway.

When leaving a limited-access highway, get into the rightmost lane. Always use your turning signals to indicate your intention to exit, and as you approach the exit ramp, slow down in the deceleration lane.

PASSING OTHER VEHICLES

Passing is a crucial part of the driving experience, and it can be done both safely or in an illegal way that endangers other road users.

Passing is always **allowed on the left** as long as you respect the rules of the road and you can execute the passing safely. The steps of safe passing are:

A. Check if there is a sign, signal, or pavement marking that prohibits passing
B. Check your mirrors first and make sure you have enough room to complete the maneuver
C. Signal your intentions via vehicle turning signals or hand turning signal
D. Change your lane smoothly and enter the passing lane
E. Accelerate to a speed that allows passing and return to your original lane only when you can see the passed vehicle's headlights in your rearview mirror

While **passing on the right is generally prohibited,** it is permissible if the roadway is unobstructed and wide enough for multiple lanes of traffic.

You can also pass on the right when the vehicle being overtaken **is either making or about to make a left turn or is on a one-way street**

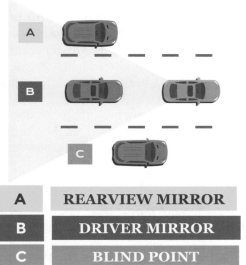

A	REARVIEW MIRROR
B	DRIVER MIRROR
C	BLIND POINT

SLOW MOVING VEHICLES

The slow moving vehicle sign is an orange triangle in the center and red on the borders. And it is more present in industrial and rural areas. The slow moving vehicles sign is for vehicles that are doing **less than 30 km/h.**

Slow-moving vehicles can be either farm equipment, horse-drawn vehicles if you are in an industrial area these will be the industrial equipment, or if you are around a marine environment another type of slow-moving vehicle will be there, and you will need to know how to handle this and identify this sign.

Sometimes vehicles with that sign move over to the shoulder of the road and sometimes they don't. If they stay on the roadway, you will have to pass, and you need to be careful when you are passing because it is one of the highest-risk crashes. Take into consideration

road markings as well, they will give you an indication of whether it is safe to pass or not. If you are not comfortable with the gap, work with a veteran driver who can help you out with judging the gap to be able to pass safely.

Following traffic blindly is a dangerous habit. This can lead to an obstructed view by a large vehicle. Also, it may result in running a red light, causing potential accidents with cross traffic.

FUNERAL PROCESSION

If you see a funeral procession on the road, **Give them the way and yield**, you should not cut in and out. All vehicles in question must have their emergency flashers and headlights on to indicate their inclusion in the procession.

Drivers within funeral processions can move through a stop sign or a red traffic light if the leading vehicle does so while the traffic light is green. Nevertheless, Funeral processions **must always yield to emergency vehicles**.

STOPPING DISTANCE

Your stopping distance is the distance a vehicle travels from the moment a driver perceives the need to stop until the vehicle comes to a complete halt. In many cases, drivers do not realize how long it takes to stop while travelling at a certain speed.

Calculating stopping distance :

Stopping distances can come in a matter of seconds that determine if you will be able to stop or not in time of hazard. It is a better practice to calculate the distance and time required to stop the vehicle.

This practice can reduce the risk of an accident if made correctly while getting more experienced as a driver this will become a second nature, that's why experienced drivers brake on time.

You can estimate the elements that enable a total stopping distance via this formula :

	Perception distance
+	Reaction distance
+	Braking distance

= **TOTAL STOPPING DISTANCE**

Perception time is the time it takes a driver to understand a situation and realize he needs to stop. Human judgment upon encountering a hazardous situation varies from one person to another. Drivers need **around 1.5 seconds** to observe a hazard and acknowledge its presence.

Nevertheless, eye health, exhaustion, and impaired driving can **increase** your perception time.

Reaction time is based on human reflexes and quick judgment upon encountering hazardous situations. On average, a driver requires about **one second** to initiate a physical response, lifting their foot off the accelerator and applying the brakes.

However, distractions, inexperience, driving under the influence of drugs or alcohol, and exhaustion can **increase** reaction time.

Braking time, A vehicle's braking time is determined by the time it takes the vehicle to stop once applying the brakes. The total distance traveled by the vehicle during this time period is considered as the **braking distance**. The speed of travelling, the condition of your vehicle tires, the weather, and the road play a major role in extending the braking time. Your tires affect your vehicle's stopping distance. Measure both the pressure and tread depth regularly and before long journeys. Always remember that **When stopping, you should begin braking early.**

DRIVING IN LOW VISIBILITY CONDITIONS

Driving during the day in comparison to driving at night poses distinct challenges and differences primarily due to variations in visibility, lighting conditions, and potential hazards.

In the Province of Alberta, make sure to switch on your headlights between **half an hour of sunset and half an hour of sunrise,** and at any other time when **visibility is low**.

OVERDRIVING YOUR HEADLIGHTS

When you drive so quickly that your stopping distance is greater than what your headlights can see, you are overdriving your headlights.

This is a risky maneuver since you may not leave yourself enough space to come to a safe halt. Reflective road signs might also deceive you by making you assume you can see further than you actually can. If you are not careful, you may over-drive your headlights.

TURN ON HEADLIGHTS

Turning on **the high beam** will significantly improve your visibility, but they are only appropriate on roads with **low or regular oncoming traffic**.

They **must be switched off** to prevent you from dazzling other drivers in **concentrated areas** such as towns and cities that have street lighting and here you do not need to use high beams.

When driving on sunny days or in situations where other drivers have not been considerate and use their high beams then perform the following steps. Look downwards towards the **right side** of the road. **Focus on the edge of the lane** and avoid looking directly ahead until the vehicle or sun glare passes.

LOWBEAM HEADLIGHTS

First, there are low-beam headlights. These are located at the front of the vehicle and are used most during the night. They point downwards which is why they are also called "dipped headlights", in essence, they reduce the possibility of dazzling other drivers at night. You may also use them whenever visibility is low.

FOG LIGHTS

Front and rear fog lights help drivers see better in **adverse weather.** Not all vehicles are equipped with front fog lights, but nearly all vehicles have rear fog lights installed. Front fog lights are located on the lowest front bumper and come in pairs. A fog light switch is found inside the cabin and can be switched on **during foggy weather** or where there is rain or heavy mist. They should however be switched off when the visibility has improved, as there is a risk of dazzling other drivers.

HIGHBEAM HEADLIGHTS

Full-beam headlights give drivers the most visibility in nighttime conditions or unlit areas. They light straight ahead instead of pointing downwards and only should be used when the road is not lit by street lights. All drivers are required to dim their headlights **within 150 meters of an oncoming vehicle**, which is approximately "one block", and **60 meters when following** another vehicle.

EMERGENCY FLASHERS

When you switch on your emergency lights, all four turning lights illuminate at the same time in a repeated rhythm. But the emergency lights should only be used in the following situations: If your vehicle is not working as it should. You need to pull over, switching your emergency lights on will show other road users that you **have an emergency** and It will allow other drivers to see you from a distance, so **they can plan** their next move.

Another situation for emergency lights in some provinces/states (when allowed) is during **a funeral procession**. Often funerals use slow-moving vehicles, and the emergency lights warn other drivers about the procession.

TURNING LIGHTS

 Your turning lights are used when you want to turn left or right. They are located on each corner of the vehicle, with some models having additional turning lights on the wings or mirrors. Their primary function is to tell other people (drivers and pedestrians) that you are turning left or right soon. This allows other drivers to **adjust their position** accordingly.

Ensure that you use your turning lights **within 30 meters** of executing the maneuver. Too early may mean that you are informing drivers of a closer turning than intended, too late and other drivers **will not have enough time to react** or know what your next move will be.

YOUR TIRE'S CONDITION

Sometimes a tire can blow which could be alarming. The signs that your tire has blown include **shaking of the vehicle, sudden loud noise**, and the vehicle generally becomes hard to drive. A driver should take extra caution with steering and focus on **driving in a straight line** as much as possible. Then slowly take your foot off the accelerator to slow down carefully. Turn on your emergency lights to inform other drivers that you will be stopping soon, and steer into the right lane, pulling over as soon as it is safe.

Inspecting your tires regularly for wear is vital to ensure your vehicle is safe. Sometimes you may experience a **shaking steering wheel** when driving **at higher speeds**. This could indicate an **unbalanced wheel**.

Every time a tire is replaced, the technician will use a wheel balancing machine to ensure the rotation of the wheel is smooth. The machine will inform the technician that a weight is needed to balance the wheel rotation and ensure your vehicle drives smoothly.

when a vehicle's tires lose traction with the road surface, **this is called a skid**, and the common causes of skidding are sudden acceleration or deceleration, harsh braking when the roadway is wet, and sharp turns at a high speed, when this happens, you can recover by Steering in the direction you want to go and easing off the accelerator and braking gently. **Hydroplaning** occurs when the tires lose contact with the road due to water, leading to loss of control. This is common in wet conditions. Drivers should reduce speed and avoid sudden maneuvers to minimize the risk.

Regularly inspecting your tires and checking for damage, uneven wear, and cracks is important as any damage could cause problems when braking or during harsh cornering, If the vehicle's tire pressure is too low, then it's harder to steer and avoid objects. If it's too high then less rubber is in contact with the road. Both under and over-pressured tires will increase your stopping distance.

Sometimes these weights can be incorrect or simply fall off when driving. **Causing an imbalance**. When this occurs, take your vehicle into a workshop for inspection. The technician can take a look at all four wheels and the suspension system to diagnose the fault and recommend steps to fix it.

6

<u>Section 1</u>

Road signs

Q1/ This traffic sign indicates that

A. No right turn is allowed
B. No left turn is allowed
C. U-turn is not allowed
D. A U-turn is allowed only if there is no traffic jam

Q2/ This traffic sign indicates that

A. Children are playing in a residential area and to drive safely
B. You are entering a school zone
C. Direction sign for employees
D. Work zone warning

Q3/ This traffic sign indicates that

A. You are entering a housing Area
B. You are entering a horse racing event
C. You are entering a helicopter airport
D. You are entering a hospital

Q4/ This traffic sign indicates that

A. No bicycles are authorized on this road at any time
B. Bumpy roads ahead
C. Do not stand or stop in this area
D. School area

Q5/ This traffic sign indicates that

A. A zoo is ahead
B. Hunting animals is permitted in this area
C. Deer regularly cross, be alert for animals
D. Deer are welcome

Q6/ This traffic sign indicates that

A. A road turns right then left
B. You need to keep to the right of the traffic island
C. You need to keep right of the obstacle
D. A winding road is ahead

Q7/ This traffic sign indicates that

A. You cannot enter
B. An uncontrolled intersection is ahead
C. A railway crossing is ahead
D. A pedestrian crossing is ahead

Q8/ This traffic sign indicates that

A. Ongoing construction, drive responsibly
B. A divided highway ends
C. A narrow bridge is ahead
D. A divided highway begins

Q9/ This traffic sign indicates that

A. Workers are on the road ahead
B. This is a construction sign, slow down and obey the flagman's direction
C. A construction sign replacing flagman on duty
D. Regulatory sign, reduce speed

Q10/ This traffic sign indicates that

A. This is an Advanced warning of danger
B. No parking is allowed starting at the arrows to the corner
C. A lane usage road sign authorizing right turn only
D. A lane usage road sign allowing all turns

Q11/ This traffic sign indicates that

A. A stop sign is located 150 metres ahead
B. A railway crossing is ahead
C. A bump is located 120 metres ahead
D. A traffic light is ahead

Q12/ This traffic sign indicates that

A. Bicycles are authorized on this road
B. No bicycles are allowed on this road
C. No parking is allowed
D. Vehicle stopping is not allowed

Q13/ This traffic sign indicates that

A. A stop sign is ahead, slow down, and drive through the intersection with caution
B. You need to slow down, if it's necessary, yield the right of way to approaching vehicles
C. You should stop and yield to pedestrians and passing vehicles from both directions
D. Proceed with caution and yield to vehicles coming from the right

Q14/ This traffic sign indicates that

A. A bus station is ahead
B. A tramway station is ahead
C. This lane
D. You are entering a side road that has no outlet

Q15/ This traffic sign indicates that

A. Slippery conditions occur when wet
B. You must share the road with oncoming traffic
C. You need to drive with caution
D. No standing is permitted

Q16/ This traffic sign indicates that

A. You are entering a route to an airport
B. You are entering an air show ahead
C. Airplanes can land in the area ahead
D. None of the options above

Q17/ This traffic sign indicates that

A. End of a 50km/h zone
B. Maximum speed in the curve is 50km/h
C. Speed limit on rural school zones
D. Speed limit will change ahead to a maximum of 50km/h

Q18/ This traffic sign indicates that

A. An intersection is straight ahead
B. A right turn is not allowed
C. Going straight is allowed
D. Driving straight through the intersection isn't permitted

Q19/ This traffic sign indicates that

A. Paved surface ends ahead
B. Pavement can become slippery when the roads are wet
C. Pavement has been milled, adhere to speed limits
D. Slowdown to avoid aquaplaning

Q20/ This traffic sign indicates that

A. A stop sign is ahead
B. You are alerted of a slow-moving vehicle
C. A dead-end street is ahead
D. A yield sign is ahead

Q21/ This traffic sign indicates that

A. A narrow road is ahead
B. An intersection is ahead
C. A hidden intersection is ahead
D. A railway crossing is ahead

Q22/ This traffic sign indicates that

A. The driver must turn right
B. Traffic may only travel in one direction
C. Keep to the right of the traffic island
D. Sharp bend or turn in the road ahead

Q23/ This traffic sign indicates that

A. Stop, then enter the traffic quickly
B. Speed up and force your way into traffic
C. Stop, and enter traffic slowly
D. Slow down, stop if necessary, and yield the right of way

Q24/ This traffic sign indicates that

A. No left turns are allowed
B. No U-turns are allowed
C. A hidden intersection is ahead
D. Lane merging from the right side. vehicles coming from both roads are equally responsible to merge

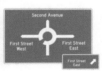

Q25/ This traffic sign indicates

A. A direction to nearby towns and cities
B. An upcoming roundabout and information about directions
C. An upcoming railway crossing
D. Distances to neighbouring towns

Q26/ This traffic sign indicates that

A. No right turns on red
B. Right turn allowed on red
C. A narrow bridge is ahead
D. No right turn is permitted

Q27/ This traffic sign indicates that

A. The Pavement narrows are ahead, drive safely
B. The right lane ends ahead, merge into the left
C. A Lane ahead is closed for roadwork.
D. Divided highway ends, traffic travels in both directions

Q28/ This traffic sign indicates that

A. Ahead you may find a snowmobiles repair shop
B. Snowmobiles parking
C. Snowmobiles may use this road
D. Snowmobiles cannot use this road

Q29/ This traffic sign indicates that

A. A divided highway ends
B. A narrow road
C. A temporarily closed road
D. Drawbridge ahead (*Bridge that lifts or swings to allow boats to pass*)

Q30/ This traffic sign indicates that

A. keep to the right if you are driving slowly on multi-lane roads
B. You need to follow the detour marker and keep to the right
C. Don't exit the highway
D. Exit the highway to the right

Q31/ This traffic sign indicates that

A. Keep the recommended distance between vehicles
B. There is a newborn baby in the vehicle ahead
C. There is a new driver in the car
D. You are coming to a highway

Q32/ This traffic sign indicates that

A. A road becomes slippery when wet
B. A hidden intersection is ahead
C. A winding road is ahead
D. A narrow road is ahead

Q33/ This traffic sign indicates that

A. You may not park between the signs during the posted time
B. No parking at any time in this area
C. Only weekday parking is authorized
D. You may park in this area during the announced time

Q34/ This traffic sign indicates that

A. The maximum speed at night is 60km/h
B. The maximum speed in a school zone is 60 km/h
C. A maximum safe speed limit on the curve
D. The recommended speed in a construction zone

Q35/ This traffic sign indicates that

A. Lane ends ahead due to road work
B. A construction crew is ahead
C. Road is temporarily separated by a median
D. Vehicles on a multi-lane road are approaching a temporarily closed exit ramp

Q36/ This traffic sign indicates that

A. Road forks to the right
B. A highway exit
C. Take the right lane if there are 2 or more people in your vehicle
D. You must turn right, the road ends ahead

Q37/ This traffic sign indicates that

A. A pedestrian crosswalk is ahead
B. A survey crew is working ahead
C. Temporary road work
D. A Person who controls the traffic is ahead

Q38/ This traffic sign indicates that

A. No parking is allowed 3.9m from here
B. Handicapped Parking
C. A winding road ahead
D. Underpass ahead. be cautious if your vehicle is over 3.9metres

Q39/ This traffic sign indicates that

A. A right lane will end ahead
B. Hidden intersection ahead
C. Passing is strictly not permitted
D. You can't pass if you are driving at a speed of 40 kilometres per hour

Q40/ This traffic sign indicates that

A. Construction zone
B. Do not enter the port area
C. Fire hall
D. There may be water flowing over the road

Q41/ This traffic sign indicates that

A. Watch for Children Crosswalk
B. During school hours and when the yellow lights are flashing obey the maximum speed limit posted on the sign
C. This is a warning sign
D. Watch for pedestrians to drive safely at a maximum speed of 40km/h

Q63/ This traffic sign indicates that

A. Vehicles approaching a bus stopping at a Bus stop need to yield once he has signalled a return to the lane
B. Yield to the right when a bus is coming
C. No bus may enter this road
D. bus may pass exclusively during daylight hours

Q43/ This Traffic Sign Indicates That

A. A railroad crossing is ahead
B. A four-way road is ahead
C. An intersection is ahead
D. A pedestrian crosswalk is ahead

Q44/ This traffic sign indicates that

A. Idling is permitted
B. No stopping for more than 3 minutes
C. No smoking
D. No idling for more than 3 minutes

Q45/ This traffic sign indicates that

A. Hidden driveway on the right
B. All Trucks enter ahead on the right
C. Bus entrance ahead on the right
D. Bus company on the right

Q46/ This traffic sign indicates that

A. The road will end ahead, you must turn to the left road
B. There is a sharp bend or turn ahead
C. You must keep to the left, traffic must exist
D. Left turn is temporarily not allowed

Q47/ This traffic sign indicates that

A. You should not enter between the times and dates mentioned
B. No stopping is allowed
C. No buses are authorized to drive in this lane
D. This lane is exclusively reserved for a certain type of vehicle and during certain days and time

Q48/ This traffic sign indicates that

A. You need to yield the right of way in the intersection ahead
B. Roundabout ahead
C. Do not enter this road
D. Two-way road

Q49/ This traffic sign indicates that

A. A narrow bridge is ahead
B. A divided highway begins
C. A divided highways ends
D. A bumpy road is ahead

Q50/ This traffic sign indicates that

A. Parking is not authorized
B. A hazard sign, the downward line reveals the side on which you can safely pass
C. Roundabout ahead drive responsibly
D. Ambulance parking only

Q51/ This traffic sign indicates that

A. A construction zone is ahead
B. A bridge or viaduct is ahead
C. Bumpy or uneven road is ahead
D. A factory is ahead, drive responsibly

Q52/ This traffic sign indicates that

A. A Railway crossing is ahead
B. Hazardous road ahead
C. You can't pass if you are driving at a speed of 40km/h or more
D. You can't switch lanes into or out of a HOV lane in this area

Q53/ This traffic sign indicates that

A. Facilities that are accessible by wheelchair
B. Lane reserved for special needs
C. Yield right of way to those with special needs
D. All of the above answers are correct

Q54/ This traffic sign indicates that

A. As the shoulder is not completely paved, do not leave the pavement
B. You need to reduce your speed and move onto the shoulder
C. move onto the shoulder at high speed
D. To increase your following distance

Q55/ This traffic sign indicates that

A. A bumpy road is ahead
B. Large trucks should drive at 18% of the normal speed limit
C. Pavement ends 18 feet ahead
D. A steep hill is ahead

Q56/ This traffic sign indicates that

A. You need to share the road with motorists, provide some space
B. This is a guide for drivers to pass the sharp curves safely
C. The Lane ahead is closed due to roadwork.
D. End of the highway, the exit is ahead

Q57/ This traffic sign indicates that

A. A paved surface ends ahead
B. A school zone is ahead
C. Do not block the intersection
D. Watch for falling rocks

Q58/ This traffic sign indicates that

A. Police, mobile radar detector ahead
B. A Survey crew working on the road ahead
C. An officer who manages traffic is ahead, follow his instructions
D. watch out for pedestrians. Also, be prepared for a merge of the road with upcoming traffic

Q59/ This traffic sign indicates that

COMMUNITY
SAFETY
ZONE
FINES
INCREASED

A. School zone area, fines increased
B. It is not safe to enter this area
C. Fines increase for G1 drivers
D. Be aware of pedestrians and the maximum speed in this area

Q60/ This traffic sign indicates that

A. Highway ahead
B. Rest area route
C. Divided highway begins
D. Road curves right

Q61/ This traffic sign indicates that

A. No littering is allowed , fine may be up to $500
B. No parking is allowed , fine may be up to $500
C. No hitchhiking is allowed , fine may be up to $500
D. Community safe zone fines may increase up to $500

Q62/ This traffic sign indicates that

A. A dangerous sharp turn is ahead
B. A dangerous road ends soon
C. A winding road ahead
D. You need to keep to the Left

Q42/ This traffic sign indicates that

A. You should not stop in the space between the signs
B. You should not stand in the space between the signs
C. You should not park in the space between the signs
D. Dangerous goods aren't allowed on this route

Q64/ This traffic sign indicates that

A. A construction work is one kilometre ahead
B. Entering the construction zone
C. The construction zone is 1 mile ahead
D. The construction zone is one kilometre before the sign

Q65/ This traffic sign indicates that

A. You need to allow space between your vehicle and cyclists
B. No motorists are allowed on this road
C. No buses or trucks permitted
D. Cyclists crossing is ahead

Q66/ This traffic sign indicates that

A. A temporary condition sign giving a restriction notice
B. A temporary condition sign showing a detour
C. A temporary condition sign indicating a winding road
D. A temporary condition sign of a diversion in the direction of the arrow

Q67/ This traffic sign indicates that

A. Keep to the right
B. This guide warn drivers of a change in direction
C. You need to stay to the right of the centre island
D. All the above answers are wrong

Q68/ This traffic sign indicates that

A. Two lanes will merge ahead
B. The two lanes ahead are closed
C. There is a highway with 2 lanes ahead
D. Two or more passengers in the vehicle are required to take this lane on the highway

Q69/ This traffic sign indicates that

A. A bumpy road is ahead
B. There is a risk of falling rocks
C. Mountains are ahead
D. A risky route is ahead, reduce your speed

Q70/ This traffic sign indicates that

A. Pedestrians are not allowed on this road
B. Pedestrians are allowed on this road
C. A pedestrian crosswalk is ahead
D. Pedestrians are authorized to walk on the road

Q71/ This Traffic Sign Indicates That

A. The center lane is for two way left turn
B. Only if you are in the centre lane you are allowed to pass
C. A two way traffic on the centre lane
D. Road forks only in the centre lane

Q72/ This Traffic Sign Indicates That

A. End of the road
B. Slowdown if you are a novice driver
C. No littering
D. End of paved roads

Q73/ This Traffic Sign Indicates That

A. Don't pass the pilot vehicle and don't pace the vehicle bearing this traffic sign
B. Cars are not allowed in this lane
C. When flashing, keep to the right and drive responsibly
D. When flashing, speed is limited

Q74/ This traffic sign indicates that

A. You are coming to an all way stop
B. You are coming to a 4 way stop
C. You are coming to a controlled intersection
D. This sign warns drivers to not misinterpret the intersection as an all-way stop

Q75/ This traffic sign indicates that

A. Pedestrian crossing
B. Be prepared to stop for pedestrians
C. No passing
D. All of the answers above

Q76/ This traffic sign indicates

A. A school zone area
B. A pedestrian crosswalk
C. That pedestrians are not allowed
D. That a rest area ahead

Q77/ This traffic sign indicates that

A. Stop for school buses when its red lights are flashing
B. Pass school buses before their red lights start flashing
C. Stop for school buses when traffic lights are flashing
D. None of the above answers

Q78/ This traffic sign indicates that

A. All the pathways of the intersection ahead have stop signs in them
B. All the lanes ahead are closed
C. Restricted roadway ahead
D. An uncontrolled intersection is ahead

Q79/ This traffic sign indicates that

A. A school bus stop is ahead. Watch for kids and school buses with flashing red lights
B. A school zone is ahead
C. A University campus is ahead, watch out for upcoming traffic when the stoplight is red
D. Pass only during daylight hours

Q80/ This traffic sign indicates that

A. A work zone ahead with a flagman.
B. The lane ahead is closed due to road work
C. Increase your following distance in this area
D. You need to follow these signs until you return to the regular route

Q81/ This traffic sign indicates that

A. Multiple roundabouts ahead
B. Narrow road ahead
C. Road is separated by a median
D. All of the answers above are correct

Q82/ The flashing lights on this sign indicate that

A. The direction of an exit
B. The direction to follow
C. That traffic need to keep left
D. That passing is strictly not allowed when lights are flashing

Q83/ This traffic sign indicates

A. That an EDR is used if an unscheduled closure of a provincial highway occurs
B. That a Special lane for an ambulance or urgent needs
C. Alberta highway shield
D. All answers above are correct

Q84/ This traffic sign indicates that

A. Parking is not allowed on this road
B. Dangerous good carriers are not allowed in this road
C. Trucks are not allowed on this road
D. Snowmobiles are not allowed on this road

Q85/ This traffic sign indicates that

A. Slight bend ahead
B. Sharp bend ahead
C. Special lane entry
D. None of the answers above

Q86/ This traffic sign indicates the

A. Hours when prohibition applies for a specific type of vehicle
B. Hours when permission applies for a specific type of vehicle
C. Trucks are prohibited on this road
D. Tracks are not allowed on this lane

Q87/ This Traffic Sign Indicates That

A. Pavement is grooved
B. Slippery conditions when wet
C. No passing
D. School zone is ahead

Q88/ This traffic sign indicates that

A. An intersection ahead, the arrow shows which direction have the right of way
B. A hidden intersection is ahead
C. Traffic Island is ahead
D. An obstruction is ahead

Q89/ This traffic sign indicates that

A. A roundabout is ahead
B. A railroad crossing is 16 meters ahead
C. You are entering canadian lands 16 meters
D. A provincial highway system sign

Q90/ This traffic sign indicates that

A. Pavement surface ends on the left side of the road
B. Pavement surface ends on the right side of the road
C. Uneven pavement on the road
D. Road narrows ahead

Q91/ This traffic sign indicates that

A. You are not allowed to turn right on the red
B. You are not allowed to turn when the intersection is blocked
C. You are allowed to turn right during certain days and hours
D. You can turn right during the posted days and hours

Q92/ This traffic sign indicates that

A. Road ends ahead
B. A roundabout is ahead
C. A stop sign is ahead
D. Do not go straight

Q93/ The motorist in the vehicle ahead signals that

A. He intends to make a left turn
B. He intends to make a right turn
C. He is slowing down or stopping
D. You have his permission to pass

Q94/ This traffic sign indicates that

A. Multiple roundabouts ahead
B. A roundabout is ahead
C. Road is separated by a median
D. All of the answers above are correct

Q95/ This Traffic Sign Indicates That:

A. No pedestrians between signs including all types of vulnerable road users
B. Dangerous goods aren't allowed on this road
C. You cannot stop your vehicle in this area unless you need to load or unload a passenger or merchandise
D. All answers above are correct

Q96/ The motorist on the vehicle ahead signals that

A. He intend to make a left turn
B. He intend to make a right turn
C. He is slowing down or stopping
D. You have his permission to pass

Q97/ This traffic sign indicates that

A. Use lower gear so the engine power goes high and the vehicle speed low
B. Use lower gear to limits stress on your brakes
C. Using lower gear is often a great option in situations like towing and hilly driving
D. All of the answers above

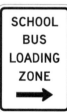

Q98/ This traffic sign indicates

A. A school bus entrance from the left
B. A zone where school buses load or unload passengers without using the red alternating lights and stop arm
C. Yield to school bus when red lights are flashing
D. A school bus detour on the left ahead

Q99/ This traffic sign indicates that

A. Facilities accessible by permit only
B. Parking is not permitted under no circumstances
C. Person with special needs transport
D. Parking is reserved exclusively for vehicles that display a valid accessible parking permit

Q100/ This traffic sign indicates that

A. A rumble strips are ahead
B. A speed hump is ahead
C. Bumpy or uneven road is ahead
D. A drawbridge is ahead

PART 1
ANSWERS :

Q1/ The Correct answer is C.
U-Turn is not allowed in the intersection ahead.

 You may find an additional plate on this sign indicating that some vehicles are excluded from the prohibition

Q2/ The Correct answer is B.
You are entering a school zone. Other signs indicating that you are entering a school area or school zone crossing are:

Q3/ The Correct answer is D.
You are entering a hospital. Blue square signs are generally guide signs indicating services along the roadway.

Q4/ The Correct answer is C.
Do not stand in this area. Standing means that you may not stop your vehicle in this area except while loading or unloading passengers

Q5/ The Correct answer is C.
Deer regularly cross. Other warning signs may indicate that other animals may cross. They may also have a supplementary plates indicating that at night danger increases.

Q6/ The Correct answer is C.
Keep right of the obstacle such as a traffic island, obstruction or median

Q7/ The Correct answer is C. A railway crossing is ahead

Q8/ The Correct answer is D. A divided highway begins. Make sure to differentiate between the 2 signs indicating the beginning or the ending of a divided highway/road.

Q9/ The Correct answer is A.
Workers are on the road ahead

Q10/ The Correct answer is C. A Lane usage road sign authorizing right turn only

Q11/ The Correct answer is D. A traffic light is ahead.

Q12/ The Correct answer is B.
No bicycles are allowed on this road.

Q13/ The Correct answer is C.
Stop and yield the right-of-way to passing vehicles from both

 directions. A stop sign may include a supplementary plate indicating that you are in an all-way stop sign intersection. thus, the right of way rules apply.

Q14/ The Correct answer is D.
You are entering a side road that has no outlet

Q15/ The Correct answer is B.
You must share the road with oncoming traffic.

Q16/ The Correct answer is A.
You are entering a route to an airport

Q17/ The Correct answer is D.
Speed limit will change ahead to a maximum speed of 50km/h

Q18/ The Correct answer is D.
Driving straight through the intersection isn't permitted

Q19/ The Correct answer is B. Pavement can become slippery when the roads are wet

Q20/ The Correct answer is B. You are alerted of slow-moving vehicles that are required by law to use a sign on their rear of the vehicle or the caravan if they are incapable of reaching speeds above 40 km/h

Q21/ The correct answer is B. An intersection is ahead

Q22/ The correct answer is B. Traffic may only travel in one direction

Q23/ The correct answer is D. Slow down, stop if necessary, and yield the right of way

Q24/ The correct answer is B. Lane merging from the right side. vehicles coming from both roads are equally responsible to merge

Q25/ The correct answer is B. An upcoming roundabout and information about directions

Q26/ The correct answer is A. No right turns on red

Q27/ The correct answer is B. A Right lane end is ahead. merge with traffic to the left. The signs bellow can also be used to indicate the ending of the right or the left lane and if it is due to temporary conditions the sign will be orange

Q28/ The correct answer is C. Snowmobiles may use this road

Q29/ The correct answer is D. Drawbridge ahead lifts or swings to allow Boats to pass.

Q30/ The correct answer is B. keep to the right if you are driving slowly on multi-lane roads

Q31/ The correct answer is C. There is a new driver in the car

Q32/ The correct answer is C. Winding road indicate a section of road with 3 or more curves. The sign will show in which direction the curves flow

Q33/ The correct answer is A. You may not park between the signs during the posted time

Q34/ The correct answer is C. A maximum speed limit on the curve You might also see them on a stretch of road that is hilly or which suddenly narrows. Yellow speed signs serve as a warning. Although they are not regulatory they provide advisory instructions to help you drive safely

Q35/ The correct answer is B. Vehicles on a multi-lane road are approaching an exit ramp which is temporarily closed

Q36/ The correct answer is A. Road forks to the right

Q37/ The correct answer is D. A Person who controls the traffic is ahead

Q38/ The correct answer is D. Underpass ahead. Take caution if your vehicle is over 3.9 metres

Q39/ The correct answer is C.
Passing is strictly not permitted

Q40/ The correct answer is D.
water may be flowing over the road

Q41/ The correct answer is B.
During school hours and when the yellow lights are flashing obey the speed limit mentioned on the road sign.

Q42/ The correct answer is A.
Vehicles approaching a bus stopping at a Bus stop need to yield once he has signalled a return to the lane

 Parking involves leaving a vehicle stationary for a more extended period

 Stopping refers to bringing a vehicle to a halt, usually for a short duration

 Standing refers to a temporary stop where the driver remains in the vehicle, ready to move, and the duration is usually short

Q43/ The correct answer is A. A railroad crossing is ahead. Other roadside that indicate that you are coming to a railway crossing or a side road are:

Q44/ The correct answer is D.
No idling for more than 3 minutes

Q45/ The correct answer is D.
Bus entrance ahead on the right

Q46/ The correct answer is B.
There is a sharp bend or turn ahead a 90 degree curve indicate that the bend is sharp rather than a slight bend. You may also find signs that indicate that you are coming to a double sharp bend

Q47/ The correct answer is D.
This lane is exclusively reserved for a certain type of vehicle and during certain days and time

Q48/ The correct answer is C.
Do not enter this road

Q49/ The correct answer is C. A divided highway/road often via median ends. make sure to differentiate between the 2 signs indicating the beginning or the ending of a divided highway/road (compare question 8 & 49). You may find also a sign that indicate that a divided road begins while both roads travel in the same direction

Q50/ The correct answer is B.
An object marker sign indicating that you are approaching objects within and immediately adjacent to the pavement that constitutes a hazard to passing traffic. the downward line reveals the side on which you can safely pass.

Q51/ The correct answer is C.
Bumpy or uneven road is ahead

Q52/ The correct answer is D.
You can't switch lanes into or out of a high occupancy vehicle lane in this area

Q53/ The correct answer is A. Facilities that are accessible by wheelchair

Q54/ The correct answer is A. This sign warns you about a soft shoulder. The dirt on the side of the road is soft. Don't leave the pavement except in an emergency.

Q55/ The correct answer is D. A steep hill is ahead

Q56/ The correct answer is A. You will need to share the road with motorists, Thus providing some space

Q57/ The correct answer is A. A paved surface ends ahead

Q58/ The correct answer is A. A Survey crew working on the road ahead

Q59/ The correct answer is D. Be aware of pedestrians and the maximum speed allowed in this area

Q60/ The correct answer is D. Road curves right

Q61/ The correct answer is A. No littering is allowed, fine may be up to $500

Q62/ The correct answer is A. A dangerous sharp turn is ahead. These types of signs with a checkerboard border are only authorized to indicate an abrupt and dangerous sharp turn or double sharp turn discontinuities or terminations.

Q63/ The correct answer is A. You should not stop in the space between the signs. Make sure to understand the difference between Stopping, Standing & Parking.

Q64/ The correct answer is A. A construction work is one kilometre ahead

Q65/ The correct answer is A. You need to allow space between your vehicle and cyclists

Q66/ The correct answer is D. A temporary condition sign showing a diversion in the direction of the arrow, other signs have a checkerboard borders which mean that the diversion can be dangerous

Q67/ The correct answer is B. A chevron alignment sign emphasizes and guides drivers through a change in horizontal alignment

Q68/ The correct answer is D. Two or more passengers in the vehicle are required to take this lane on the highway

Q69/ The correct answer is B. There is a risk of falling rocks

Q70/ The correct answer is A. Pedestrians are not allowed on this road

Q71/ The correct answer is A. The center lane is for two-way left turns

Q72/ The correct answer is A. End of the road

Q73/ The correct answer is A. Don't pass the pilot vehicle and don't pace the vehicle bearing this traffic sign

Q74/ The correct answer is D.
This sign warns drivers to not misinterpret the intersection as an all-way stop

Q75/ The correct answer is D.
All of the answers above

Q76/ The correct answer is B. A pedestrian crosswalk

Q77/ The correct answer is A.
Stop for school buses when its red lights are flashing

Q78/ The correct answer is A.
All the pathways of the intersection ahead have stop signs on them

Q79/The correct answer is A. A school bus stop is ahead. Watch for kids and school buses with flashing red lights

Q80/ The correct answer is D.
You need to follow these signs until you return to the regular route

Q81/ The correct answer is B.
Narrow road ahead

Q82/ The correct answer is B.
This sign displays the direction to follow

Q83/ The correct answer is C.
Alberta Highway shield

Q84/ The correct answer is B.
Dangerous goods carriers are not allowed

Q85/ The correct answer is A.
Slight bend ahead

Q86/ The correct answer is A.
Hours when prohibition applies for a specific type of vehicle

Q87/ The correct answer is A.
Pavement is grooved

Q88/ The correct answer is A.
An intersection is ahead and the arrow shows which direction have the right of way

Q89/ The correct answer is D. A provincial highway system sign

Q90/ The correct answer is C.
Uneven pavement on the road

Q91/ The correct answer is C.
You are allowed to turn right during certain days and hours

Q92/ The correct answer is C. A stop sign is ahead

Q93/ The correct answer is C.
He is slowing down or stopping

Q94/ The correct answer is A.
A roundabout is ahead

Q95/The correct answer is C.
You may not stop your vehicle except to load or unload passengers or merchandise

Q96/ The correct answer is A.
He intends to make a left turn

Q97/ The correct answer is D.
All of the answers above

Q98/ The correct answer is B. A zone where school buses load or unload passengers without using the red alternating lights and stop arm

Q99/ The correct answer is D.
Parking is reserved exclusively for vehicles that display a valid accessible parking permit

Q100/ The correct answer is B.
A speed hump is ahead

7

Section 2
Rules of the road

Q01/ When driving at the posted speed limit during nighttime, what factor increases the risk compared to daytime driving?

A. At night, your reaction time is four times slower
B. At night, your braking time is four-time slower
C. At night, you cannot see very far ahead
D. Some drivers have made it illegal to drive with just their parking lights on

Q02/You are considered legally intoxicated in the Province of Alberta if your blood alcohol level is _____ or above.

A. 0.6
B. 0.06
C. 0.8
D. 0.08

Q03/ On multilane roads, if your intention is to drive slower than the flow of traffic, in which lane you should drive

A. The middle lane
B. The rightmost lane
C. The leftmost lane
D. You can drive in any lane if you respect the posted speed limits

Q04/ Who has the right of way at a roundabout

A. Vehicles who prepare to exit the roundabout
B. Large vehicles over small vehicles as they have wide blind spots
C. Vehicles on the right
D. Traffic already at the roundabout

Q05/ Which insurance coverage of the following is mandatory?

A. Third-party liability
B. Comprehensive coverage
C. Collision coverage
D. Liability damage to non-owned automobile

Q06 / You are coming to an intersection where traffic lights are not working, how would you manage this situation?

A. Yield to traffic from your left side only before proceeding
B. Yield to traffic from your right side only before proceeding
C. If traffic lights are not working this means that there is no reason for traffic control therefore you have the right of way at all times
D. Treat this situation as if you are entering an all-way stop sign junction

Q07/ Reducing speed solely to observe accidents or any unusual occurrences.

A. Can prevent rear-end accidents
B. Can lead to a better traffic flow
C. Demonstrates defensive driving behaviour
D. Will lead to traffic congestion

Q08/ What factors can influence your blood alcohol content?

A. The amount of alcohol you've consumed
B. Your fitness level
C. The type of alcohol you've been drinking
D. Your height to weight ratio

Q09/ A solid yellow line marked on the pavement indicates that

A. The road that you travel on is a one-way road
B. The road that you travel on allows you to travel in one direction only
C. You can't cross this line to pass or turn
D. You can cross this line to pass or turn

Q10/ Flaggers or flagmen are usually located in which area to optimize the flow of traffic

A. In construction areas and highways
B. At school zones
C. At a controlled intersection
D. At an uncontrolled or blind intersection

Q11/ Before leaving your vehicle parked on the right side of the street facing a downgrade, you should

A. Leave your front wheels parallel to the curb
B. Set your parking brake only
C. Turn your front wheels to the left and set your parking brake
D. Turn your front wheels to the right and set your parking brake

Q12/ At an intersection where a pedestrian is crossing and the traffic lights switch from red to green, what should you do

A. Yield to the pedestrian and allow them to complete their crossing.
B. Safely proceed as you have the right of way.
C. Use your horn to alert the pedestrian to give you the way.
D. Blame the pedestrian for crossing slowly

Q13/ What are the tell-tale signs that the pedestrian crossing the intersection is blind

A. They often wear an orange hat and a black sunglass
B. They are often guided by a family member or a friend hence they can be easily identifiable
C. The usage of guide dogs and orange canes
D. The usage of guide dogs and white canes

Q14/ In which situations can you execute a left turn on a red light?

A. Only from a two-way street onto another two-way street
B. Only when the intersection is blocked
C. Only from a one-way street onto another one-way street
D. At your own discretion regardless of the street type

Q15/ What is the role of a shared center lane

A. Reserved for vehicles that have a special permit
B. Parking or stopping
C. Making a right turn onto a major thoroughfare
D. Making two-way left turns

Q16/ If your parked car unintentionally rolls and collides with another unattended vehicle, what should you do?

A. Activate your horn to alert others to the situation
B. Move your car and carry on with your journey
C. Notify the police about the incident

Q17/ Shoulder checks are an essential defensive skill because

A. They are the best move to communicate your intentions of changing lanes and help you determine who is driving behind you

B. They are crucial to alert oncoming vehicles of hazards or emergency situations

C. They will assist you while changing lanes, as regardless of your mirror's adjustment, there will always be a blind spot

D. All of the answers above are correct

Q18/ You are driving and you encounter an intersection where the stoplight is red, but you have instructions from a police officer signalling you to proceed

A. Obey the officer's instructions by proceeding

B. Stop to see what other drivers doing before making a decision

C. Wait for the stoplight switch to green

D. Alert the officer that he is not paying attention to the colour of the light

Q19/ When is the proper moment to switch on the vehicle's headlights?

A. There is no specific time

B. Between sunset and dawn, and at any other time when visibility is less than 150 metres

C. Between a half-hour after sunrise and a half-hour before sunset, or at any other time when visibility is low (less than 150 metres)

D. From sunset until dawn

Q20/ Hands-free devices may include

A. phone/hand-held wireless communication device used to text or dial

B. hand-held electronic entertainment devices, (Ex: a tablet/portable gaming console)

C. display screens unrelated to driving

D. All of the above

Q21/ What is the best decision a driver can make to avoid skidding?

A. Apply the brakes firmly

B. Steer straight ahead

C. Steer in the direction you want to go

D. Steer in the opposite direction of the skid

Q22/ When you find yourself in an intersection and hear the siren of an emergency vehicle, what should you do?

A. Move to the right and stop at the intersection

B. Continue through the intersection, then pull over to the left and stop

C. Move to the left and stop at the intersection

D. Continue through the intersection, then pull over to the right and stop

Q23/ What is the best course of action if you miss your exit on an interstate highway?

A. Continue to the next exit.

B. Stop and ask for help.

C. Back up to reach your exit.

D. Make a U-turn to reach your exit

Q24/ What should you do if you and another vehicle arrive at an uncontrolled intersection at the same time?

A. It's up to you to choose who goes first because there is no specific right-of-way law in this situation.
B. The vehicle on the right has the right of way in this scenario.
C. The vehicle on the left has the right of way in this scenario.
D. The vehicle with the loudest horn

Q25/ What is the first thing to do if you are the first person to come upon the scene of a collision

A. Move injured bodies off the road
B. Call the local authorities and ask for an ambulance if needed
C. exchange insurance information
D. Call the injured person's family or friends

Q26/ What is a true characteristic of roadways on bridges and overpasses during cold, wet weather?

A. They have a tendency to freeze earlier than the rest of the road
B. They do not freeze because they are constructed from concrete
C. They tend to freeze at the same time as the rest of the road
D. They usually freeze after the rest of the road does

Q27/ To maintain a safe gap between the vehicles ahead of you, how far behind them should you drive?

A. The one second rule
B. The two second rule
C. The three second rule
D. The four second rule

Q28/ As per the Alberta Motor Vehicles Insurance Act, the minimum insurance required for third-party liability is:

A. $100,000
B. $300,000
C. $200,000
D. $400,000

Q29/ In a situation where 2 vehicles cross paths on a steep mountain, who is granted the right of way?

A. The ascending vehicle
B. Both vehicles
C. The descending vehicle
D. They should wait for a law enforcement officer to facilitate the passage of both vehicles

Q30/ What do we call the areas in which you are not visible to the driver in front?

A. A Blind Spot
B. A No-Zone area
C. A construction area
D. A Rear-view area

Q31/ While driving through an intersection, what message does a red light followed by a green arrow convey?

A. You are allowed to proceed in all directions except the one indicated by the arrow
B. This traffic control signal allows pedestrians to cross the intersection. Treat this situation as a yield sign
C. You are allowed to proceed in the direction the arrow indicates without stopping

Q32/ The Graduated Driver Licensing (GDL) program will improve road safety

A. Creating a complex environment full of difficult tasks for all new drivers.
B. Creating an uncontrolled, high-risk environment for all new drivers.
C. Creating a lower risk, controlled environment for all new drivers.
D. Providing minimal support in an uncontrolled environment for all new drivers.

Q33/ If another vehicle creates a hazard by suddenly cutting in front of you. What should be your initial course of action among these choices??

A. Take your foot off the gas
B. Sound your horn and step on the brake firmly
C. Swerve into the lane next to you
D. Drive onto the shoulder

Q34 /What does a law require you to do before entering the intersection at a red light and making a right turn :

A. Stop, then edge into traffic.
B. Stop, signal, and make the turn so as not to interfere with other traffic including pedestrians
C. Slow down and proceed with caution.
D. Slow down, signal and turn.

Q35/ Flashing amber and red lights on a vehicle indicate

A. A goods vehicle ahead
B. A construction vehicle ahead
C. A long-haul truck ahead
D. A snow plow ahead

Q36/When it is safe to do so, passing vehicles on the right side is

A. Not a permitted maneuver under any circumstances
B. Allowed on any street or highway
C. Allowed when a street or highway has two or more lanes for traffic in the direction you are travelling to and the passing can be done safely, or on one-way roads
D. Allowed if you want to overcome from the right edge of the road

Q37/Following commercial vehicles too closely is a dangerous decision because

A. Commercial vehicle drivers are less competent
B. Commercial vehicles are not predictable
C. They have wide blind spots
D. They often carry dangerous goods

Q37/ You need to leave at least a _____ distance while passing a cyclist.

A. 3 metres
B. 2 metres
C. 1.5 metre
D. 1 metre

Q38/ When lights are required, drivers must use High-beam headlights

A. Within a 300-metre of a passing vehicle
B. At their discretion. This is a precautionary measure, not a law
C. At 150 metres from an oncoming vehicle or 60 meters when following a vehicle
D. Within 100 metres of an oncoming vehicle

Q39/ You are approaching an intersection where traffic lights are not functioning. How should you handle this situation?

A. Yield to traffic from your left side only before proceeding
B. Yield to traffic from your right side only before proceeding
C. If traffic signals are not working, it means there is no reason for traffic control, so you have the right of way at all times.
D. Treat this situation as if you are entering an all-way stop sign junction

Q40/Which of the following statements is true for child restraints?

A. Children under the age of six years and whose weight does not exceed 18 kg must be restrained in a child safety seat
B. Children under the age of seven years and whose weight does not exceed 19 kgs must be restrained in a child safety seat
C. Children who is under the age of nine years and whose weight does not exceed 25 kgs must be properly restrained in a child safety seat
D. Any child who is under the age of eight years and whose weight does not exceed 20 kgs must be properly restrained in a child safety seat

Q41/ What is the speed limit by default in school zone areas?

A. 50km/h
B. 30km/h
C. 20km/h
D. 15km/h

Q42/ Flashing yellow lights indicate that you should

A. Treat the intersection as a stop sign intersection, meaning you should stop and give the right-of-way
B. Proceed without stopping as you have the right to do so
C. Treat the intersection as a yield sign, meaning you should slow down and stop if necessary and give the right-of-way
D. Stop and wait for the light to turn green before proceeding

Q43/ If you come up on several snowplows clearing a freeway, you should not

A. Wait for the plows to allow traffic to safely pass
B. Try to pass between them
C. Keep a safe distance
D. Do any of the above

Q44/ What should you do if you receive a call when operating a vehicle

A. Pullover and park before answering the call.
B. Answer immediately to know what is happening.
C. Answer the phone only if you are expecting an important call.
D. Text back and say that you are driving and therefore you can't answer the call.

Q45/Generally when speed limitation isn't posted, the maximum speed allowed in cities, towns and villages is

A. 50 km/h
B. 60 km/h
C. 40 km/h
D. 30 km/h

Q46/ If you are at a red light and the intersection is blocked, what is the appropriate action to take when the light turns green?

A. Proceed cautiously, ensuring your chances of clearing the intersection are high
B. Stop until the intersection is no longer blocked by traffic, then proceed
C. Sound your horn to encourage other vehicles to move quickly
D. Make a U-turn and change your roadway, helping to clear the blocked intersection

Q47/ On a two-lane, two-way road, a _____ allows you to cross over into the opposing lane temporarily to pass a vehicle if it is safe to do so.

A. Left arrow
B. Solid white line
C. Broken yellow line
D. Solid yellow line

Q48/ The maximum speed limit on roadways located outside of the urban areas is

A. 90 km/h
B. 70 km/h
C. 100 km/h
D. 80 km/h

Q49/ Which statement from the following is a crucial parking rule?

A. Do not park on a Highway
B. Never park close to a fire hydrant
C. Never Park on a curve or bend
D. A, B & C are all correct, therefore D is the right answer

Q50/ What is a detour and what is the purpose of it?

A. A high occupancy vehicle lane or road
B. An interstate/province highway
C. A high-speed tollway
D. A temporary alternative roadway to avoid congestion or bypass a closed road

Q51/ When a streetcar is stopped to pick up or discharge passengers and there is a safety island, what does the law require you to do?

A. Pass on the left side of a streetcar
B. Pass with caution and be ready to stop if a pedestrian makes a sudden or unexpected move
C. Stop at least two metres behind the safety island
D. Sound your horn and pass with caution

Q52/ Unbalanced tires are due to which problem from the following?

A. Weak shock absorbers
B. Not having enough fuel
C. Using the ABS excessively
D. Uneven distribution of weight around the tire

Q53/ When turning left at an intersection, it is important to give priority to:

A. Traffic behind you
B. Traffic on the right side
C. Traffic coming from the opposite direction
D. You don't have to yield to anyone

Q54/ What is the best precautionary action to do if you are blinded by an oncoming vehicle high beam lights during the night while driving

A. Change your lane immediately
B. Sound your horns and alert the driver
C. Use your high beam as well so he will understand that he is causing discomfort to other drivers
D. Look at the right side of the road

Q55/ There are two lines in the center of the road dividing traffic. One is a solid line while the other is a broken one. the line on your side is solid

A. This line divides traffic travelling in opposite directions
B. It is safe to pass and overtake
C. Passing is not allowed
D. You can only make a U-turn

Q56/ If you and the driver on your left arrive at an intersection with stop signs on all four corners simultaneously, who has the right of way?

A. The driver on your left the right of way
B. You have the right of way
C. Whoever is courteous can give it
D. Whoever is signalling to make a turn has the right of way

Q57/ Which type of accidents is the most frequently observed on interstates?

A. Head-on collisions
B. Commercial vehicle accidents
C. Side collisions
D. Rear-end collisions

Q58/ By law you are required to follow the instructions from

A. A security guard at a residential area
B. A parent at a school zone
C. A flagger at a construction area
D. A, B & C are all correct, hence D is the right answer

Q59/ If someone is tailgating you?

A. Keep your distance and get out of the way
B. Move into another lane when it is safe to do so
C. Slow down slightly to increase the space in front of your car
D. any of the above

Q60/ Exceeding the posted speed limit so you can overcome another vehicle is

A. Generally allowed if this maneuver can be done safely
B. Allowed only on interstate highways and rural areas
C. Not allowed under any circumstances
D. Allowed only if you are an experienced G class driver

Q61/ In wintry or icy driving conditions, which actions are recommended?

A. Utilizing your cruise control is a safe practice
B. Modify your speed and turns with extra caution, compared to normal conditions
C. You should drive just as you would in regular weather
D. Accelerate your speed for better control

Q62/ The total stopping distance of the passing vehicle can be calculated as

A. The ratio between reaction distance and braking distance
B. The sum of perception distance, reaction distance and the braking distance of the vehicle
C. The difference between the perception distance, reaction distance and braking distance of the vehicle
D. The average of perception distance and braking distance

Q63/ You can also earn demerit points for breaking traffic laws in?

A. Outside of the country
B. All of north America
C. Other provinces in Canada
D. All of the preceding

Q64/ What is the best measure to prevent hydroplaning?

A. Reduce your speed in adverse weather conditions.
B. Make certain that your vehicle's tires have good tread depth.
C. Make sure that your vehicle's tires are properly inflated with the required tire pressure.
D. A, B, and C are all correct, thus D is the right answer

Q65/ In areas with playing children while driving, expect:

A. Their awareness of safe crossing
B. Stopping at the curb before crossing
C. Potential sudden, inattentive running in front of your vehicle
D. Crossing only when with an adult

Q66/ How does marijuana affect a driver's ability to respond to sights and sounds?

A. It enhances their ability to respond to sights and sounds
B. It does no effect on their responsiveness
C. It makes it more difficult for them to respond to sights and sounds, lowering their ability to handle a quick series of tasks
D. It only affects their response to expected events

Q67/ What information from the following isn't important to exchange before a collision?

A. Making sure both parties agree about who is at fault.
B. Full name and contact information of parties involved.
C. Insurance policy information.
D. Driver's license information.

Q68/ What is the minimum time period required to complete both the learner's and probationary stages of the GDL program?

A. Three years
B. Five years
C. Four years
D. Seven years

Q69/ Safely backing includes all the following measures expect

A. Looking over your rearview mirrors
B. Alerting traffic of your intentions
C. Checking behind your car before you get in
D. Tapping your horn before you back up

Q70/ What is the meaning of a red arrow signal at a junction?

A. You can turn in the arrow's direction
B. You must stop and wait for pedestrians to cross
C. Do not turn in the direction of the arrow and wait for a green signal or arrow
D. You can proceed with caution without waiting for a signal change

Q71/ The likelihood of Collision tends to increase when

A. All vehicles are travelling near or at the same speed
B. One line of the traffic is travelling much slower than the others
C. Where there is a traffic jam
D. One vehicle is travelling faster or slower than the flow of traffic

Q72/What should you do when you park your vehicle facing uphill next to a curb?

A. Set the hand brake and keep the wheels straight
B. Set the hand brake and turn the wheels toward the curb
C. Set the hand brake, also turn your wheels away from the curb
D. Put the transmission in first gear

Q73/ According to Alberta Laws and regulations, how close to a fire hydrant can you legally park?

A. Around 2 metres
B. Around 5 metres
C. Around 3 metres
D. Around 10 metres

Q74/ On a wet road, you must quickly stop your vehicle. To stop a vehicle that doesn't have ABS, the simplest solution is to:

A. Engage the handbrake and deactivate the ignition.
B. Reapply the brake if the wheels begin to lock up.
C. Squeeze the brakes.
D. Keep the window down and provide a signal.

Q75/ Class 7 licence holders are subject to zero alcohol levels and are not permitted to drive

A. During the day time
B. During afternoon hours
C. From 11 p.m. to 12 p.m.
D. From midnight to 5 a.m.

Q76/ On streets and roads, what use do broken white lines serve?

A. They denote a "no-stop" zone.
B. They facilitate the separation of vehicles in opposing directions.
C. They denote a no-parking zone.
D. They divide traffic travelling in the same direction and indicate that passing is authorized.

Q77/Who has the right of way if three vehicles arrive at an intersection with an all-way stop sign?

A. The vehicle which comes to the intersection first.
B. The vehicle turning left.
C. The vehicle on the left.
D. The vehicle that turning right.

Q45/ If your breath test shows an alcohol concentration level between 0.05 and 0.08%, which of the following consequences will you be subject to for your first offence?

A. You will be fined.
B. Your licence will be suspended for 3 days.
C. Your vehicle will be towed.
D. All of the above.

Q79/ When a police officer signals you to pull over, what is your legal obligation?

A. Immediately stop your vehicle in the current lane of travel
B. Gradually and safely come to a full stop by moving to the right side of the road
C. Politely decline the officer's request and accelerate your vehicle.
D. If you have a legitimate reason, ensure a complete stop of your vehicle

Q80/ If a driver is involved in an accident and overall damages exceed $2,000, he/she should

A. Call the police and remain at the scene
B. Call the police and leave the scene
C. Not report the accident to the police
D. Work with other drivers to clear the accident scene

Q81/ What causes skid on the road?

A. Slippery roads
B. Acceleration
C. Outdated tires
D. All of the above

Q82/ When driving behind a large truck on the freeway, what is the recommended approach?

A. Maintain a closer following distance compared to a passenger vehicle
B. Keep a greater following distance than you would for a passenger vehicle
C. Pass the truck promptly on its left side
D. Pass the truck swiftly on its right side

Q83/ Parking close to a curve is prohibited because

A. You will need to pay the meter first
B. Because it is designated for loading shipment
C. It is reserved for disabled people parking
D. You will block the visibility of other road users and create more hazards on the road

Q84/ Overdriving your headlights is risky because

A. It is not good for the car battery.
B. You are driving too fast.
C. Your headlights are too bright
D. You cannot stop within the distance that you can see

Q85/ The crucial aspect to bear in mind when it comes to managing speed on curved roads is

A. Maintain the posted speed limit as you approach the curve, then reduce speed at the sharpest part
B. Decelerate before entering the curve
C. Gradually increase speed before entering the curve

Q86/When lights are required, drivers must switch from high-beam lights to low beams when following another vehicle.

A. Within 30 meters
B. Within 120 meters
C. Within 60 meters
D. This only applies when approaching another vehicle

Q87/ Why driving under the influence of alcohol or any other substance or medication is a very dangerous habit

A. It will slow your perception and reaction time
B. It will make you obnoxiously confident and ego-driven
C. It will influence negatively the safety of roadways
D. A, B & C are all correct, hence D is the right answer

Q88/ What does the law say about passing from the right side

A. It is not allowed under any circumstances
B. Allowed on residential areas to avoid congestion
C. Allowed on school zone areas to avoid congestion
D. You can pass on the right if you are passing a vehicle making a left turn and can do it in a safe manner

Q89/ Snow removal vehicles on public roadways are equipped with flashing _____ lights.

A. Orange
B. Red
C. Yellow
D. Blue

Q90/ Which of the following situations makes a U-turn unsafe and illegal?

A. If the driver's vision is impeded by a bridge, ramp, or tunnel, within 150 metres.
B. In a bend, with a clear view in either direction of 150 metres.
C. In a railway crossing, or within 30 metres of a railway crossing
D. In all the aforementioned circumstances.

Q91/ You may lend your issued driver's license to another driver

A. If he has an immediate emergency
B. If his driving privilege is suspended
C. If you are confident of his driving skills
D. Under any circumstances

Q92/ During adverse weather conditions such as fog rain or snow you are required to

A. Use your emergency flashers for better vision
B. Use your low-beam headlights for better vision
C. Use your parking lights for better vision
D. Use your horns to communicate your intentions

Q93/ When going down a steep hill while driving a manual transmission what should you do

A. turn on your emergency flashers
B. keep applying your brakes
C. shift into a higher gear
D. shift into a lower gear

Q94/ If you are involved in an accident in which someone is injured, you must?

A. Report the accident at once to the nearest provincial municipal police officer
B. Report the accident within 48 hours to the nearest provincial or municipal police officer
C. Report the accident to your insurance company only
D. Report the accident to the Ministry of Transportation

Q95/ If suddenly one of your tires blows out, you should

A. Take your foot of the gas pedal to slow down
B. Bring the vehicle to stop off the road
C. Concentrate on steering
D. A, B, and C are all correct, thus D is the right answer

Q96/ What is the speed limit by default in the school zones in the province of Alberta?

A. 50km/h
B. 30km/h
C. 20km/h
D. 15km/h

Q97/ Why it's crucial to check for motorcycles before changing lanes?

A. Motorcycles are often difficult to spot due to their compact size.
B. Motorcycles are typically granted priority at intersections
C. Motorcycles are known for excessive speed.
D. Sharing traffic lanes with motorcycles is prohibited by law

Q98/ When driving behind a large commercial vehicle, you must make sure that you can see

A. Both its side mirrors
B. Its left-hand side mirror
C. Its right-hand side mirror
D. Its registration plate

Q99/ When driving in slow, heavy traffic and approaching a railroad track before an upcoming intersection, what should you do?

A. Wait until you can completely clear the railroad tracks before continuing
B. Stop just before the crossing gates in case they should close
C. Stop on the tracks until there is room in the intersection beyond them
D. Proceed cautiously, seeking an alternate route if possible

Q100/ In an uncontrolled intersection scenario where two drivers approach simultaneously from opposite directions—one proceeding straight and the other making a left turn—which vehicle holds the right-of-way?

A. Both of the vehicles are first required to come to a halt and then proceed.
B. The vehicle which is turning on the left side has the right-of-way.
C. Both of the vehicles have the right of way.
D. The vehicle which is going straight is considered to have the right-of-way

PART 2
ANSWERS :

Q01/ The answer is C. It is riskier to drive at the maximum speed limit at night than it is during the day due **to reduced visibility**.

Q2/ The answer is D. You are legally intoxicated in Alberta if your blood alcohol level **(BAC) is 0.08%** or above.

Q03/ The answer is B. For better traffic management and to avoid congestion **use the rightmost lane** to avoid interrupting the traffic flow.

Q04/ The answer is D. Traffic already at the roundabout has the right of way over traffic that is trying to enter.

Q05/ The answer is A. the third party liability is mandatory in the province of Alberta.

Q06/ The answer is D. Treat the intersection as if it were **controlled via a stop sign**, meaning that you should **obey the right-of-way rules.**

Q07/ The answer is D. Avoid slowing down to look at accidents on the roadways, as **it interferes with the smooth flow of traffic**

Q08/ The answer is A. Different types of drinks have no different effects on you. It is **the amount of alcohol** you consume that elevates your blood alcohol concentration.

Q09/ The answer is C. Yellow solid lines convey two major pieces of information to road users, Firstly, they indicate that the line **separates traffic travelling in opposite directions**. Secondly, the fact that the line is solid, regardless of its colour, signifies that **passing or turning is strictly prohibited.**

Q10/ The answer is A. Flaggers are present at construction sites to **optimize traffic flow** and help drivers **avoid hazards.** you are required by law to follow their instructions.

Q11/ The answer is D. Turn your front wheel to the right and set your parking brake

Q12/ The answer is A. Even if the traffic lights turned green **the pedestrian still has the right of way** and he should complete his crossing. Driving requires courtesy and discipline!

Q13/ The answer is D. The usage of guide dogs and white canes marks the presence of a blind pedestrian. This situation requires extra prudency and alertness from drivers, **especially the ones driving an electric or hybrid vehicle** as blind pedestrians rely on sound to identify their presence.

Q14/ The answer is C. You are permitted to make a left turn at a red light. However, this is only allowed when you're on **a one-way street intending to enter another one-way street** with no prohibiting signage. Always exercise caution and yield to pedestrians while proceeding.

Q15/ The answer is D. A shared center lane is distinguishable via double yellow lines, one set of broken yellow lines on the inside, and solid yellow lines on the outside.

And is designated **for executing left turns or U-turns where permitted**

Q16/The answer is C. You are required to report the collision, adhering to the legal obligation of notifying authorities within 24 hours of its occurrence.

Q17/ The answer is C. It is vital to quickly glance over your shoulder while changing lanes to identify vehicles in your blind spot regardless of how you adjust your mirrors.

Q18/ The answer is A. Law enforcement officers, such as police or peace officers **should be obeyed over traffic control signals and signs** for better traffic management and safety. They have the authority to direct traffic and override the usual rules when necessary.

Q19/ The answer is C. Between half an hour after sunset and half an hour before dawn, and at any other time when visibility is less than 150m.

Q20/ The answer is D. Hands-free devices feature all the aforementioned options.

Q21/ The answer is c. Lift your foot from the accelerator and shift to neutral, avoiding an immediate attempt to steer. Allowing the wheels to skid sideways will gradually reduce the vehicle's speed, restoring traction. Then, steer in the direction you want to go

Q22/ The answer is D. Avoid **obstructing an intersection**, even when an emergency vehicle is on its way. If you're in an intersection and you hear or see an emergency vehicle approaching, proceed through the intersection first. henceforth, pull over to the right at the earliest safe opportunity and come to a stop.

Q23/ The answer is A. **Never stop, back up, or try to turn in** an interstate highway as it will create a dangerous driving situation

Q24/ The answer is B. The vehicle **on the right has** the right of way under these circumstances. To add, pedestrians and other vulnerable road users have the same driving privileges.

Q25/ The answer is B. Call the local authorities and ask for an ambulance if needed

Q26/ The answer is A. They tend to freeze before the rest of the road does.

Q27/ The answer is B. The **two-second** rule refers to the minimum guideline for the following time.

Q28/ The answer is C. The minimum amount limit in third-party liability coverage is 200.000 CAD.

Q29/ The answer is A. The vehicle travelling downhill must **yield the right-of-way by backing up**

Q30/ The answer is D. The general term used to describe the area in which you are not being seen by a driver upfront unless he performs a shoulder check is called a blind spot. It is situated on his back right and left side.

Q31/ The answer is C. This combination of signals indicates that you are only allowed to proceed in **the direction indicated** by the green **arrow** without stopping.

Q32/ The answer is C. Creating a lower risk, controlled environment for all new drivers.

Q33/ The answer is A. Taking your foot off the gas will allow your car to slow gradually while you maintain a firm grip on the steering wheel. Do not take any other action until your vehicle has slowed

Q34/ The Answer is B. Stop, signal, and make the turn so as not to interfere with other traffic including pedestrians

Q35/ The answer is D. A snow plow ahead

Q36/ The answer is C. Allowed when a road has 2 or more lanes for traffic in your direction and the passing can be done safely

Q36/ The answer is C. No amount of **blood alcohol concentration is allowed** for drivers under 21 as part of the zero-tolerance law

Q37/ The answer is C. They have wide blind spots

Q38/ The answer is C. At 150 metres from an oncoming vehicle or 60 meters when following a vehicle

Q39/ The answer is D. Treat this situation as if it were a **four-way stop sign**, meaning that you should stop and yield to the vehicle

Q40/ The answer is A. Any child who is under the age of six years and whose weight does not exceed 18 kgs must be properly restrained in a child safety seat.

Q41/The answer is B. 30km/h

Q42/ The answer is C. Treat the intersection **as a yield sign**, meaning you should slow down and stop if necessary and give the right-of-way

Q43/ The answer is B. You should not pass between them.

Q44/ The answer is A. Always pull over and park before answering the call unless you are answering from a hands-free device

Q45/ The answer is A. 50km/h.

Q46/ The answer is B. As a wise driver, you are responsible for making roadways safe, This is why the best decision to make where traffic flow is congested on intersections is to remain calm, **not proceed until the junction is cleared**, and then you can go. Making a U-turn can be unsafe in such circumstances and sounding your horns can lead to an aggressive reaction from irresponsible road users.

Q47/ The answer is D. On a two-lane, two-way road, **a broken yellow** line indicates that you are allowed to cross over into the opposing lane

Q48/ The answer is D. 80 Km/h

Q49/ The answer is D. All of these statements are correct because they can create hazards on the road and the likelihood of collisions.

Q50/ The answer is A. A temporary alternative roadway to avoid congestion or bypass a closed road.

Q51/ The answer is B. Pass with caution and be ready to stop if a pedestrian makes a sudden or unexpected move

Q52/ The answer is D. **Uneven distribution of weight** around the tire can lead to the pulling of the vehicle on one side of the road, vibration, and increased fuel consumption.

Q53/ The answer is C. You are required to give the right of way to vehicles coming from the opposite direction.

Q54/ The answer is D. In such circumstances, look at the right side of the road and avoid a direct look at the lights.

Q55/ The answer is C. It is not considered safe to pass or turn left

Q56/ The answer is B. You have the right of way as both vehicles arrived at **the same time** and you are **on the right**

Q57/ The answer is D. **Rear-end collisions** are the most frequent crashes on interstates

Q58/ The answer is C. You are required by law to follow the **instructions of a flagger** at a construction zone to avoid hazards and congestion during unusual road conditions.

Q59/ The answer is A. Keep your distance and get out of the way

Q60/ The answer is B. Exceeding the posted speed limit is not allowed under any circumstances

Q61/ The answer is B. **Reduce** your speed and turns with extra caution

Q62/ The answer is B. The sum of perception distance, reaction distance and the braking distance of the vehicle

Q63/ The answer is B. You will also gain demerit points if you commit any traffic offence in Other provinces in Canada

Q64/ The answer is D. All of the options are correct.

Q65/ The answer is C. In areas with playing children, while driving you should expect Potential sudden, inattentive running in front of your vehicle

Q66/ The answer is C. Smoking or eating marijuana **impairs a driver's ability to respond to sights and sounds,** making them less capable of handling quick tasks and significantly decreasing their responsiveness, especially when facing unexpected events on the road.

Q67/ The answer is A. While it's crucial to exchange, determining fault is **a matter for insurance companies** and authorities to decide based on the available evidence.

Q68/ The answer is A. Three years

Q69/ The answer is D. Tapping your horn isn't a necessary measure and sometimes can be a misplaced gesture

Q70/ The answer is C. A red arrow signal at an intersection indicates that **you are not allowed to turn in the direction of the arrow**.

Q71/ The answer is D. On the opposite hand, collisions shall tend to decrease if all the vehicle maintains the same speed limit on the road

Q72/ The answer is C. Point your wheels away from the curb and then roll back slowly so that the rear part of the right front wheel rests against the curb. The curb **will block your car from rolling backward** if your brakes fail.

Q73/ The answer is B. According to Alberta Laws and regulations, never park closer than 5 meters to a fire hydrant

Q74/ The answer is B. Reapply the brake if the wheels begin to lock up. You should be able to bring yourself to a complete stop in your lane

Q75/ The answer is D. From midnight to 5 a.m.

Q76/ The answer is D. Broken white lines (dashes) are used to divide traffic travelling in the same-direction and indicate that changing lanes is authorized.

Q77/ The answer is A. The drivers need to yield the right-of-way to the vehicle that comes first at the stop sign.

Q78/ The answer is A. The type of car seat is determined by looking at the age and/or weight of a child. It is vital that all of the child car seats fall under the safety standards and are well secured.

Q79/ The answer is B. Gradually and safely come to a full stop by moving to the **right side** of the road

Q80/ The answer is C. Call the police and remain at the scene

Q81/ The answer is D. All of the above.

Q82/ The answer is B. Large trucks have **wider blind spots**. Thus, you need to drive with extra caution alongside commercial vehicles

Q83/ The answer is D. You will block the visibility of other road users and create more hazards on the road

Q84/ The answer is D. You cannot stop within the distance that you can see

Q85/ The answer is B. Always **Decelerate** before entering a curve

Q86/ The answer is C. Within 60 meters

Q87/ The answer is D. All of the aforementioned answers are correct

Q88/ The answer is D. You can pass on the right if you are passing a vehicle making a left turn and can do it in a safe manner

Q89/ The answer is D. Snow removal vehicles have flashing blue lights.

Q90/ The answer is D. The 4 answers above are examples of instances in which doing a U-turn is unsafe or illegal.

Q91/ The answer is D. Your driver's license is personal and can't be shared under any circumstances

Q92/ The answer is B. In conditions of reduced visibility use your **low-beam headlights** for better vision.

Q93/ The answer is D. Ease off the accelerator and downshift to a lower gear. This action will create a braking effect, slowing down the vehicle, a technique known as **engine braking**

Q94/ The answer is A. Report the accident at once to the nearest provincial municipal police officer In case you are willing to make a claim, ensure that the important information is shared with the driver, and also do not forget to get in touch with your insurance company promptly.

Q95/ The answer is D. A, B, and C are all correct, thus D is the right answer

Q96/ The answer is B. 30km/h, The speed limits in school zone areas become more than numbers; they transform into a shield against unforeseen hazards.

Q97/ The answer is A. It is crucial to be vigilant and look carefully for motorcycles when changing lanes **because their smaller size can make them less visible** to other drivers

Q97/ The answer is C. Yield to vehicles as you are merging to make your maneuver safer.

Q98/ The answer is A. Both its side mirrors

Q99/ The answer is A. Never cross the railroad track unless there is room on the other side. Navigating a railroad crossing demands a heightened sense of caution from drivers

Q100/ The answer is D. In case the two vehicles enter an uncontrolled intersection simultaneously from opposite directions, the vehicle going straight is considered to have the right-of-way.

Made in United States
Troutdale, OR
10/09/2024